Sub-Roman Britain (AD 400-600)

A gazetteer of sites

Christopher A. Snyder

BAR British Series 247
1996

Published in 2019 by
BAR Publishing, Oxford

BAR British Series 247

Sub-Roman Britain (AD 400-600)

© Christopher A. Snyder and the Publisher 1996

The author's moral rights under the 1988 UK Copyright,
Designs and Patents Act are hereby expressly asserted.

All rights reserved. No part of this work may be copied, reproduced, stored, sold, distributed, scanned, saved in any form of digital format or transmitted in any form digitally, without the written permission of the Publisher.

ISBN 9780860548249 paperback
ISBN 9781407318745 e-book

DOI https://doi.org/10.30861/9780860548249

A catalogue record for this book is available from the British Library

This book is available at www.barpublishing.com

BAR Publishing is the trading name of British Archaeological Reports (Oxford) Ltd. British Archaeological Reports was first incorporated in 1974 to publish the BAR Series, International and British. In 1992 Hadrian Books Ltd became part of the BAR group. This volume was originally published by Tempvs Reparatvm in conjunction with British Archaeological Reports (Oxford) Ltd / Hadrian Books Ltd, the Series principal publisher, in 1996. This present volume is published by BAR Publishing, 2019.

BAR titles are available from:

        BAR Publishing
        122 Banbury Rd, Oxford, OX2 7BP, UK
EMAIL   info@barpublishing.com
PHONE +44 (0)1865 310431
FAX   +44 (0)1865 316916
        www.barpublishing.com

CONTENTS

LIST OF ILLUSTRATIONS	4
LIST OF ABBREVIATIONS	4
PREFACE	5

PART I: THE NATURE OF THE EVIDENCE

Introduction	6
Identifying Ethnicity in the Archaeological Record	6
Dating Sites: Coinage, Pottery, and Scientific Methods	6
Notes	9

PART II: GAZETTEER OF SITES

The East	14
Canterbury	14
Chelmsford	15
Chichester	15
Colchester	15
London	16
Portchester	17
Richborough	17
St. Albans	18
The Southwest	19
Bantham	19
Bath	19
Brean Down	20
Cadbury-Congresbury	20
Cannington	21
Castle Dore	21
Chun Castle	22
Dorchester/Poundbury	22
Exeter	23
Glastonbury	23
Ham Hill	24
High Peak	24
Killibury	25
Lundy Island	25
Maiden Castle	25
Nettleton	25
Phillack	26
The Scilly Isles	26
Shepton Mallet	26
South Cadbury	26
Tintagel	28
Trethurgy	29
Wells	29
West Hill Uley	30
Winchester	30
Wales	31
Aberffraw	31
Breiddin/New Pieces	31
Caerleon	31
Caernarvon	31
Caerwent	32
Caldey Island	32
Capel Maelog	33
Coygan Camp	33
Degannwy Castle	33
Dinas Emrys	34
Dinas Powys	34
Dinorben	35
Gateholm	36
Glan-y-Mor	36
Graenog	36
Longbury Bank	37
Ty Mawr	37
The Midlands	38
Bourton-on-the-Water	38
Chester	38
Cirencester	39
Droitwich	40
Frocester	40
Gloucester	40
Milton Keynes	41
Silchester	41
Wall	42
Worcester	42
Wroxeter	43
The North	44
Ancaster	44
Ardwall Isle	44
Binchester	45
Buston	45
Carlisle	45
Catterick	46
Doon Hill	46
Dumbarton Rock	46
Hadrian's Wall	47
Lincoln	48
Mote of Mark	49
Ravenglass	49
Whithorn	50
Yeavering	50
York	51
Notes	51
BIBLIOGRAPHY	64

ILLUSTRATIONS

Fig. 1	Distribution of Sites in Sub-Roman Britain: Definite, Probable, and Possible.	12
Fig. 2	Distribution of Sites by Type in Late and Sub-Roman Britain.	13
Fig. 3	Map of Sites in the East.	14
Fig. 4	Map of Sites in the Southwest.	19
Fig. 5	Map of Sites in Wales.	31
Fig. 6	Map of Sites in the Midlands.	38
Fig. 7	Map of Sites in the North.	44

ABBREVIATIONS

BAR	British Archaeological Reports.
BBCS	*Bulletin of the Board of Celtic Studies.*
Bede, *EH*	Bede, *Ecclesiastical History of the English People.*
CBA	Council for British Archaeology.
CIIC	*Corpus Inscriptionum Insularum Celticarum.*
CIL	*Corpus Inscriptionum Latinarum.*
CMCS	*Cambridge/Cambrian Medieval Celtic Studies.*
ECMW	*Early Christian Monuments of Wales.*
ECMS	*Early Christian Monuments of Scotland.*
HMSO	Her Majesty's Stationery Office.
LPRIA	Late Pre-Roman Iron Age.
PSAS	*Proceedings of the Society of Antiquaries of Scotland.*
RIB	*Roman Inscriptions of Britain.*
RIC	*Roman Imperial Coinage.*

PREFACE

Sub-Roman Britain (AD 400-600): A Gazetteer of Sites is meant to be used as a quick-reference tool for archaeologists and historians studying late Roman and early medieval occupation in Britain. "Sub-Roman" is here used strictly chronologically to refer to the fifth and sixth centuries AD, not as a cultural or artistic label denoting degeneracy from Roman forms. Geographically, "Britain" refers to the once-Roman area of the island of Britain, from the Forth-Clyde line to the Isles of Scilly. While the Gazetteer attempts to include all sites within these parameters which have shown strong evidence of occupation in the fifth and sixth centuries, preference has been given, in this edition at least, to sites exhibiting some evidence of continuity of occupation from the Iron Age and/or Roman periods. Entirely new settlements, of both Irish- and Germanic-speaking peoples, will hopefully be added to the database in subsequent print and electronic editions. (An electronic edition of the Gazetteer is being prepared for *Internet Archaeology*, which can be found on the World Wide Web at http://intarch.york.ac.uk.)

Although I have added personal commentary and form to the Gazetteer, much of my work has involved the collection and editing of excavation reports and archaeological surveys. I am thus deeply indebted to the hundreds of archaeologists whose fieldwork and publications have gone into the making of this Gazetteer. I thank them all collectively, and invite their participation in the future expansion of the database. I would especially like to thank Prof. Stephen D. White for his encouragement and advice, and my editor, Dr. Rajka Makjanić, for her enthusiastic support of this project. The following individuals receive my gratitude for reading and commenting upon various parts of this study: Thomas S. Burns and David F. Bright (Emory University); Patrick Wormald (Oxford University); and W.R. McLeod (West Virginia University). I would also like to thank Chuck Spornick and Marie Hansen of the Woodruff Library (Emory University) for their invaluable help, and the staff members at the following institutions for their assistance: the Swem Library (College of William and Mary); the University of Georgia Library; the Institute for Historical Research and the British Library (London); the Ashmolean Museum Library (Oxford); the Cambridge University Library; the National Library of Wales (Aberystwyth); the University of Glasgow Library; and the Edinburgh University Library, the National Library of Scotland, and the Library of the Museum of Antiquities (Edinburgh). Financial support for study and travel was graciously provided by Emory University; the English Speaking Union of America (Atlanta Branch); the Frank Berry Memorial Trust; the St. Andrew's Society of Washington, DC; and the Council of Scottish Clans and Associates. Lastly, I would like to express my appreciation for the editorial assistance given by Mr. Ben Horter and my wife, Renée Baird Snyder. *Et Deo gratias*.

Chris Snyder
Williamsburg
September, 1995

PART ONE: THE NATURE OF THE EVIDENCE

Introduction

"The darkest of the Dark Ages" might be an apt description of the fifth and sixth centuries in Britain, a time commonly referred to as the sub-Roman period. Not dark in the sense that this era lacked character or achievement: there are certainly enough real (St. Patrick) and legendary (Arthur and Merlin) associations to attract modern interests. Anyone who has investigated the history of the period behind these figures, however, soon discovers the exasperating dearth of contemporary written records. Further study only leads to agnosticism, and indeed it may be that we will never be able to write a narrative history of sub-Roman Britain.

The slack has fortunately been taken up by archaeologists. The material culture of the fifth and sixth centuries, though itself not extensive, is in many ways more accessible than the problematic written sources. At first, archaeology was used merely to supplement historical models which relied chiefly on the testimony of writers like Gildas, Bede, and Nennius.[1] After a profusion of source criticism began to shake these foundations,[2] however, many archaeologists felt free to ignore the written record entirely and treat sub-Roman Britain as a prehistoric subject.[3] The pendulum now seems to be swinging back toward the middle, with the most recent archaeological surveys of the period attempting a balance between speculative archaeological models and careful use of the written sources.[4]

These latest surveys are notable contributions and will undoubtedly influence the direction of future archaeological speculation. Yet there is something noticeably missing from this growing body of scholarship. Kenneth Dark puts his finger on it:

> It is sadly true that no two modern surveys of the settlement archaeology of the period have managed to agree on a common corpus of sites.... The situation has resulted in an exceptionally unstructured data-base, chaotic in its randomness and often in the arbitrariness with which sites are included or excluded in discussion.[5]

There has, in fact, never been an attempt to present the database in a single comprehensive format. Even the most thorough of the surveys have at best presented only a handful of sites, and those only when they strengthen a particular argument which the author is trying to make. There are some excellent regional catalogs and gazetteers,[6] and Dark has himself presented much of the data in his recent work on site identification.[7] Yet, as valuable as these resources are, they do not fill the need for a single, comprehensive reference tool for researching individual sites and settlements in sub-Roman Britain.

The Gazetteer in Part Two of this study is an attempt to fill this void. It will no doubt suffer the typical failings of first attempts at constructing an archaeological reference tool: site omissions, dated material, incomplete excavation reports. But instead of begging the readers' forgiveness, I shall instead extend an invitation for reader response and cooperation in the future expansion and revision of the database.

Identifying Ethnicity in the Archaeological Record

The nature of the archaeological evidence for sub-Roman Britain poses several problems. One is our ability, or more often inability, to identify "ethnicity" in the archaeological record. Structures, coins, pottery, jewelry, and military equipment have all traditionally been used by archaeologists to identify settlements and graves as Romano-British, Celtic, Germanic, Anglo-Saxon, etc. However, all of these items can be used and reused by groups of people not necessarily responsible for their design or creation. For example, a "Roman" structure could be inhabited by "Germanic" squatters, and a "Romano-Briton" could wear "Germanic" jewelry. This has resulted in the questioning of several traditional assumptions. "Germanic" belt-buckles, for example, used to be taken as a sure sign of the presence of barbarian *foederati* in Roman Britain; now we know that they may not even indicate a military presence. In fact, the widespread early finds of "Germanic" jewelry and pottery have suggested to some scholars that the majority Britons were simply adopting the tastes of the minority Saxons, indicating a change of culture more than a change of population.[8]

There is, then, no archaeological indicator that can unquestionably define the ethnicity of a burial or settlement. However, some stylistic terms that are widely accepted and used by archaeologists for descriptive purposes—e.g. Romano-Celtic temple, Germanic pottery—will be used in the present survey.[9] Here archaeology must work with written evidence to "suggest" the continuity of a Romano-British settlement, the "re-emergence" of a native "British" community, or the appearance of a new population of barbarian settlers, be they Irish or Germanic. Imported Mediterranean pottery, penannular brooches, and Germanic *Grubenhäuser* (sunken-floored huts) are all strong indicators of ethnicity, but their importance—for this Gazetteer—rests in their ability to help date a particular site, rather than to identify its occupants with confidence as "Roman," "Briton," or "Saxon."

Dating Sites: Coins, Pottery, and Scientific Methods

Dating is a crucial problem which plagues both historians and archaeologists working in this period. The scarcity of coinage and chronological indicators in the written sources deteriorates confidence in assigning precise dates for artifacts and settlements. For this survey, I have tried to avoid precise dates for settlements; I am only concerned with whether or not activity occurred at a particular site during the fifth and sixth centuries. The means of dating sites used in the Gazetteer are, in the order of their importance, as follows: numismatic evidence (datable coins, ingots, and medallions); ceramic evidence (dishes and pottery which have been cataloged by type); various scientific dating methods (radiocarbon, archaeomagnetic), particularly those tests conducted quite recently which offer significantly enhanced precision; bonework, metalwork, glass, and jewelry dated by type or design; and dates from written sources, scarce in the sub-Roman period and almost always controversial.

The numismatic and ceramic evidence are not only indicators of date; they also provide important clues about the sub-Roman economy in Britain and its relationship to that of Rome's other former provinces. In the fourth century, currency entered Britain in the form of precious-metal coins, bullion (usually plate), and (silver) ingots. Up to 326, the mint at London was issuing bronze coinage, and for a brief period (312 and 314) it served as a comitatensian mint and issued some gold.[10] Again, from 383 to 388, London minted some gold coinage for Magnus Maximus, but at some subsequent date it ceased to operate.[11] Precious-metal currency was usually sent to Britain (after 388 from Gaul) to pay imperial servants (both civil and military), who were in turn expected to return it to the government in the form of tax payments or else exchange it for bronze coins.[12] These transactions were normally facilitated by the *nummularii* or *collectarii*, who sold the precious metals back to the government and turned a profit. Thus, gold and silver were not expected to stay in circulation for very long in the provinces, and bronze coinage became the agent for day-to-day transactions.

The amount and kind of coinage reaching Britain also fluctuated according to the purposes of the various emperors. Archaeologists studying coin frequency also have to take into account the vagaries of "coin loss," both accidental and intentional. For fourth-century Britain, a study of bronze coinage alone shows dramatic fluctuations, ending with the total cessation of new bronze issues in 402.[13] The last issues of gold and silver to reach Britain are those of Arcadius and Honorius minted in the first decade of the fifth century, along with the *solidi* and *siliquae* of Constantine III.[14] Individual finds in Britain dating later than 411 tend to be copies or counterfeit, not official issue.[15]

Thus, the picture one gets is that the Roman state was no longer providing coins to the Diocese of the Britains after the Rescript of Honorius. Does this mean, then, that coins went out of use soon after 410? The standard answer is "yes," and that the Britons therefore must have engaged only in barter economy subsequent to this date. Richard Reece, however, has come to a different conclusion by observing the numismatic evidence of the fifth century from excavations at Roman Carthage, noting that "coinage seems to be made up of worn coins of the high periods of supply in the mid-fourth century. Losses are very low, and what is lost is very poor."[16] This pattern closely parallels that of fifth-century Britain.[17] Perhaps, as many are now suggesting, older issue coins circulated throughout the fifth century—and later—along with more recent counterfeits, and those that were lost were worn because of their continued use.[18] This seems to have been the case for many areas of the sub-Roman West, resulting in a "hotch-potch" coinage (to borrow Dark's phrase), based on shape and weight rather than denomination, that continued well into the medieval period.[19]

The continuing circulation of coinage in sub-Roman Britain can be offered only as a possibility on archaeological grounds. However, the written sources provide evidence that argues strongly for this being indeed the case. Patrick mentions both *solidi* and *scriptulae* in his writings.[20] Gildas states that the priests of his day have not contributed a single *obolum* to the poor, yet they "grieve if they lose a single *denarius*; if they gain one, they cheer up."[21] And in one seventh-century Byzantine saint's life, there is an account of an Egyptian ship returning from southwestern Britain laden with *nomisma* and tin.[22]

Along with scattered losses, we must also take into account the numerous coin hoards discovered in British excavations. Hoarding coins can signify many things, including (but not limited to) the threat of barbarian invasion (or of a campaigning Roman army), a devalued currency, or simply safe-keeping in the absence of a banking system. Over 1600 hoards of Roman coins have been recorded from Britain, most containing between 100 and 300 coins, though some contain over 1000.[23] Britain betrays a unique pattern of hoarding, for gold coin hoards are almost nonexistent, while silver and bronze hoards are quite numerous.[24] There have been several recent surveys and analyses of these British hoards.[25] A look at coin distribution by emperor shows that hoards containing coins of Honorius and/or Constantine III (over 80) rank second only to the Tetrici/Gallic Empire hoards (over 100), suggesting that hoarding was popular when Britain was cut off from Rome and coinage became scarce.[26] This should not be surprising, nor should the geographic distribution of the late hoards, which Robertson has shown concentrates on eastern coastal areas where raiding was most frequent.[27]

However, it may be surprising that many of the coins in these hoards, especially the silver *siliquae*, show clear signs of "clipping," an easy means of obtaining gold and silver and also a way to create small change in the absence of reliable official bronze. These clipped coins of Honorius and Arcadius date to after 393, but this only provides a *terminus post quem* for the clipping and hoarding.[28] "The clipping of *siliquae* is a British phenomenon and requires a British explanation," declared George Boon; but a clear explanation has been elusive.[29] Given that the act of clipping was a crime punishable by death, and that few examples can be found prior to the end of the fourth century, it seems likely that this occurred in Britain when there were no longer any authorities present (or interested enough) to enforce the penalty; it also likely occurred while denomination still mattered in Britain, as opposed to the shape and weight of the coin which would be undermined by clipping. Andrew Burnett's analysis of hoards from both Britain and Ireland containing clipped *siliquae* have convinced many that the clipping probably took place during the uncertain years of the reign of Constantine III, verifying Zosimus's statement that "the Britons ceased to obey Roman laws" after 409.[30] The traditional view has been that this clipping was due to a shortage of silver coin imported from the continent during and after the usurpation of Constantine.[31] John Kent has offered the theory that "the *siliqua* was a coin used to make some habitual payment" in Britain, "and that it continued to be used for this purpose in early post-Roman times, but was then clipped to a smaller diameter because its value had become enhanced in relation to the importance of that payment."[32] Philip Grierson and Melinda Mays suggest that these coins may have been intended as half-*siliquae*, clipped by Marcus, Gratian, and Constantine to obtain silver for ingot payments to their troops, while the clipped coins could then be distributed to ordinary citizens during public appearances.[33] These are both plausible explanations for the clipping of coins during the tumultuous years of 406 to 411.

Non-systematic clipping likely continued for some time after this, though it is notable that clipped coins are usually found associated with Roman objects, while there are no recorded associations with items of post-Roman—either "British" or "Anglo-Saxon"—manufacture.[34] The deposition of these hoards then, especially in vulnerable coastal areas, is likely a fifth-century phenomenon, with a *terminus post quem* of the latest coin in each hoard.[35]

Both the hoarding of silver coins issued in the late fourth and early fifth centuries (63 hoards were recorded by Archer in 1979), and the systematic clipping of these silver coins, occur in Britain on a remarkable scale compared to the rest of Europe, and in the East these phenomena are virtually nonexistent.[36] But another type of silver-hoarding—sometimes referred to as *Hacksilber*—is common to Britain and to other areas of the West where barbarian raiding occurred in the fifth century. These hoards contain gold or (more commonly) silver plate and other valuables, and are often cut-up or otherwise damaged in their depositional state.[37] They occur both inside and outside the diocesan border in Britain, while one of the most noteworthy examples comes from Coleraine in northern Ireland.[38] The most noteworthy collections from Britain are those found at Mildenhall, Water Newton, Canterbury, Thetford, and Traprain Law. Most of these hoards are dominated by decorated silver plate of a very high quality. Some contain items with *chi-rho*s and other explicitly Christian symbols. Those found beyond the frontier, particularly the Traprain Law hoard, contain pieces that have been cut and folded. At first this was thought to represent the loot from a barbarian raid on a Roman settlement. However, recent examinations have shown that the weight of these pieces corresponds with even ratios to Roman coinage, suggesting that the items were official payments to barbarian clients or would-be clients.[39]

Official payments could, alternatively to coin and plate, also be made in foodstuffs. For example, the Roman army along the frontier needed to be supplied with grain (*annona*), which was transported over long distances in large pottery containers (*amphorae*). Commercial trade in luxury goods often followed these same official trade routes, and in the early empire these items—manufactured mostly in Gaul, Italy, and Spain—reached Britain via the rivers of Gaul and the Channel. Later, however, North Africa became the chief supplier of grain (as well as olive oil) for the empire, and North African goods were shipped accordingly in North African pottery. Study of the distribution of pottery in the later empire shows an increasing number of examples of this pottery, especially African Red Slip Ware.

Pottery is ubiquitous in Roman Britain, as indeed it is in most periods, for without it there could have been no life. Pottery also has a remarkable ability to survive in the archaeological record. In the first centuries of Roman rule, fine table wares—both locally-made and imported Samian varieties—could be found along with the imported *amphorae*. By the late fourth century, the active commercial kilns in Britain (some of which were exporting their wares to the Continent) were those producing Oxfordshire Ware, Black-Burnished Ware (from south Dorset), New Forest pottery, Alice Holt Forest pottery, Nene Valley pottery, and Crambeck Ware.[40] The traditional assumption is that these British pottery manufacturing centers had ceased operating by 410. Now, however, it is believed that the Oxfordshire kilns, the New Forest kilns, and those producing Black-Burnished Ware (I) continued to flourish for some time after the year 400.[41] Smaller, local producers of coarse wares flourished alongside the large commercial kilns throughout the Roman period, and there is much evidence that "organically-tempered" and other crude wares (e.g. grass-, shell-, calcite-, and limestone-tempered wares) were made and used throughout southern and western Britain in the fifth and sixth centuries and possibly beyond.[42] In excavated settlements where pottery is totally absent, the occupants likely used wood or leather substitutes which seldom leave archaeological traces.[43]

The decline in volume and quality of post-410 British pottery is often seen as paralleling the decline of a money economy (that is, the absence of new coins) in Britain, and to have been influenced by the absence of both the military and urban markets. However, this picture of decline and collapse is misleading. Like coins, pottery could have circulated for many years after the state-controlled production centers had closed. As for imported pottery, excavation is revealing an actual **revival** of wares in the sub-Roman period, carrying, for the most part, luxury items. These imports include not only Gaulish products coming to Britain from the old river-routes of Gaul, but also increasingly goods produced in such diverse Mediterranean centers as Byzacena, Phocaea, Cyprus, Gaza, and the cities of the Aegean, coming to Britain **directly** from such major ports as Carthage and Alexandria in the fifth and sixth centuries.

These imports were first discovered during the excavations of C.A. Ralegh Radford at Tintagel, Cornwall in the 1930s.[44] Termed colloquially "Tintagel ware," the imports soon began turning up at other newly-excavated sites in both western Britain and Ireland, though the Tintagel collection remains the largest and most diverse. Radford and subsequent excavators adopted the labels **Ai** to **Aii** and **Bi** to **Bvi** to describe the imports.[45] However, after the appearance of John Hayes's in-depth study of African Red Slip Ware and other late Roman Mediterranean wares, Charles Thomas suggested an alternative labelling scheme:

PHOCAEAN RED SLIP WARE (PRSW): Fine wares produced in western Turkey (probably Phocaea), c.500.

PHOCAEAN RED SLIP WARE—STAMPED DECORATION.

AFRICAN RED SLIP WARE (ARSW): Popular fine wares produced in North Africa (probably Carthage), late fifth to early sixth century.

AFRICAN RED SLIP WARE—STAMPED DECORATION.

Bi AMPHORAS: Wine jars produced in the eastern Aegean, mid sixth century.

Bii AMPHORAS: Wine jars produced in the eastern Mediterranean (Nubia, Cyprus, and Antioch have all been proposed), mid to late fifth century.

Bi and Bii AMPHORAS—GRAFFITI.

Biv HANDLED JARS: One- and two-handled water (?) jars produced in Asia Minor (probably Sardis), mid fifth to mid sixth century.

BYZACENA AMPHORAS (Bv): Large cylindrical oil containers produced in the Byzacena region of North Africa, late fifth century.

GAZA AMPHORAS (Bvi): Large cylindrical wine (?) containers produced at Gaza, mid fifth to mid sixth century.

B MISCELLANEOUS AMPHORAS (Bmisc).

D WARE: Grey bowls produced in the Bordeaux region, sixth century.

E WARE: Kitchenware (jars, pots, bowls, jugs, pitchers, and beakers), some pieces containing traces of purple dye. Produced in western Gaul, c.500-700.

MINOR UNIDENTIFIED WARES: Small, grey-slipped, wheel-made bowls or dishes.[47]

Thomas's labels will be used exclusively in the Gazetteer of Sites. How and why these imports came to Britain will also be discussed in the Gazetteer under the specific sites which have yielded them.

Finally, a few words must be said about the precision of the archaeological evidence for this period. The scientific cataloging and analysis of finds like coins, pottery, and jewelry is a relatively recent phenomenon, with inexact reports more typical for those sites excavated several decades ago. Even when more recent analysis could be exact, as in the case of numismatic evidence, it is seldom accomplished in excavation reports, many of which remain only in preliminary form. Given these drawbacks, the purpose of the present study is not to offer precise dates for Roman and sub-Roman occupation at particular sites. Rather, coins and pottery are used only to help place activity in the fifth and sixth centuries. If **this** can be done with confidence (the degree of which is signified by the labels "Definite," "Probable," and "Possible" in the Gazetteer), archaeologists and historians can then attempt to talk about the sub-Roman Britons in terms of their structures, weapons, jewelry, pottery, and other surviving artifacts. Once the scholarly community agrees upon at least **some** definite sub-Roman sites, the artifactual and written evidence combined will provide plenty of material for future discussion of the politics, economy, and culture of the enigmatic Britons.

Notes

[1] E.g. R.G. Collingwood and J.N.L. Myres, *Roman Britain and the English Settlements* (Oxford: Clarendon Press, 1936); Sheppard Frere, *Britannia: A History of Roman Britain* (London: Routledge and Kegan Paul, 1967); and Leslie Alcock, *Arthur's Britain: History and Archaeology AD 367-634* (New York and London: Penguin, 1971). For a more thorough survey of this archaeological tradition, see Snyder, "'The Tyrants of Tintagel': The Terminology and Archaeology of Sub-Roman Britain (AD 400-600)" (Ph.D. diss., Emory University, 1994), chaps. 1 and 12.

[2] E.g. David N. Dumville, "Sub-Roman Britain: History and Legend," *History* 62 (1977): 173-92. My critique of the written sources can be found in Snyder, *An Age of Tyrants: Britain, AD 400-600* (Univ. Park, PA: Penn State Univ. Press, forthcoming), chap. 4.

[3] E.g. C.J. Arnold, *Roman Britain to Saxon England* (Bloomington, IN: Indiana Univ. Press, 1984). For a critique of this school of thought, see Leslie Alcock, "The Activities of Potentates in Celtic Britain, AD 500-800: A Positivist Approach," in *Power and Politics in Early Medieval Britain and Ireland*, ed. S.T. Driscoll and M.R. Nieke (Edinburgh: Edinburgh Univ. Press, 1988), 22-46.

[4] E.g. Nicholas Higham, *Rome, Britain, and the Anglo-Saxons* (London: Seaby, 1992); and Kenneth R. Dark, *Civitas to Kingdom: British Political Continuity 300-800* (Leicester: Leicester Univ. Press, 1994).

[5] K.R. Dark, *Discovery by Design: The Identification of Secular Elite Settlements in Western Britain AD 400-700*, BAR British Series No. 237 (Oxford: BAR Publishing, 1994), 67.

[6] E.g. Nancy Edwards and Allan Lane, eds., *Early Medieval Settlements in Wales 400-1100* (Cardiff: Univ. of Wales Press, 1988); Lynette Olson, *Early Monasteries in Cornwall* (Woodbridge, Suffolk: Boydell Press, 1989), xiv, 41-45; Elizabeth A. Alcock, "Appendix: Defended Settlements, Fifth to Seventh Centuries A.D.," in *25 Years of Medieval Archaeology*, ed. D.A. Hinton (Sheffield: Dept. of Prehistory and Archaeology, Univ. of Sheffield, 1983), 58-59; idem, "Enclosed Places, AD 500-800," in *Power and Politics*, 40-46; and Elizabeth A. and Leslie Alcock, "Catalogue of Fortified Sites in Wales and Dumnonia, c.AD 400-800," in Leslie Alcock, *Economy, Society and Warfare Among the Britons and Saxons* (Cardiff: Univ. of Wales Press, 1987), 168-71. Though no catalog of Roman towns with sub-Roman activity has been compiled, some are included in the map of urban centers with "Fifth-century activity" in Peter Salway, *The Oxford Illustrated History of Roman Britain* (Oxford: Oxford Univ. Press, 1993), 319.

[7] Dark, *Discovery*.

[8] This theory is explored in depth in Lloyd and Jennifer Laing, *Celtic Britain and Ireland AD 200-800: The Myth of the Dark Ages* (New York: St. Martin's, 1990); and in Higham, *Rome*. Cf. Salway, *The Oxford Illustrated History of Roman Britain*, 298 (fig.), 328-29, 332 (fig.).

[9] See, for example, Niall M. Sharples, *Maiden Castle* (London: Batsford/English Heritage, 1991), 130: "They are known as Romano-Celtic temples because they are believed to represent a fusion of Celtic and classical religions."

[10] See P.J. Casey, "Constantine the Great in Britain—the Evidence of the Coinage at the London Mint," in *Collectanea Londiniensia*, ed. J. Bird *et al.*, London and Middlesex Archaeological Society Special Paper No. 2 (London: London and Middlesex Archaeological Society, 1978): 181-93.

[11] See Anne S. Robertson, *Roman Imperial Coins in the Hunter Coin Cabinet, University of Glasgow: Vol. V. Diocletian (Reform) to Zeno* (Oxford: Oxford Univ. Press, 1982), xx, 428. The London mint issued gold *solidi* for Maximus.

[12] For a description of how this worked in the military, see Richard Reece, "Mints, Markets and the Military," in *Military and Civilian in Roman Britain*, ed. T.F. Blagg and A.C. King,

BAR British Series No. 136 (Oxford: BAR Publishing, 1984), 143-60.

[13] See A.S. Esmonde Cleary, *The Ending of Roman Britain* (London: Batsford, 1989), 93, 138-39; and Richard Reece, *Coinage in Roman Britain* (London: Seaby, 1987), 23. The death of Theodosius in 395 marked an abrupt cessation of the AE 2 bronze denomination. Thereafter, only AE 3 and AE 4 were issued in the West, produced mostly by the mint in Rome. The last bronze denomination to reach Britain was the AE 4 of Honorius, issued by the Rome mint from 395-402. Cf. Philip Grierson and Melinda Mays, *Catalogue of Late Roman Coins in the Dumbarton Oaks Collection and in the Whittemore Collec-tion: From Arcadius and Honorius to the Accession of Anastasius* (Washington, DC: Dumbarton Oaks, 1992), 39-47, 207-9.

[14] J.P.C. Kent, *The Roman Imperial Coinage, Vol. X (AD 395-491)* (London: Spink and Son, 1994), lxxxv: "presumably the import and disbursement of silver [in fifth-century Britain] ceased before that of gold." Constantine III's coins were minted at Trier, Lyon, and Arles from 407 to 411 in two phases (identified by the changing number of G's in the VICTORIA AUGGG formula): the first phase (407-8) ended with the news of the death of Arcadius, the second (408-11) with the death of Constantine himself. The coins are predominantly *solidi* and *siliquae*, along with rare tremisses from Arles and half-*siliquae* and AE 4 from Lyon. *Siliquae* from Arles were also struck in the name of his son Constans c.410. See Grierson and Mays, 214-18; Esmonde Cleary, *The Ending*, 138; and Kent, "The End of Roman Britain," 21.

[15] See G.C. Boon, "Counterfeit Coins in Roman Britain," in *Coins and the Archaeologist*, ed. J. Casey and R. Reece (London: Seaby, 1987), 102-88; and M. Blackburn, "Three Silver Coins in the Names of Valentinian III (425-55) and Anthemius (467-72) from Chatham Lines, Kent," *Numismatic Chronicle* 148 (1988): 169-74.

[16] Richard Reece, "The Uses of Roman Coinage," *Oxford Journal of Archaeology* 3 (1984): 197-210 (205).

[17] Ibid., 205.

[18] See Dark, *Civitas*, 200ff.; Boon, "Counterfeit Coins," 145; idem, "Byzantine and Other Exotic Ancient Bronze Coins from Exeter," in *Roman Finds from Exeter*, ed. N. Holbrook and P. Bidwell, Exeter Archaeological Reports No. 4 (Exeter: Exeter Archaeological Reports, 1991); idem, "Theodosian Coins from North and South Wales," *BBCS* 33 (1986): 429-35; and C. Sutherland, "Coinage in Britain in the Fifth and Sixth Centuries," in *Dark Age Britain: Studies Presented to E.T. Leeds*, ed. D.B. Harden (London: Methuen, 1956), 5.

[19] See Dark, *Civitas*, 201-3; Reece, "The Uses of Roman Coinage"; and C. Morrison, "The Re-Use of Obsolete Coins: the Case of Roman Imperial Bronzes Revived in the Late Fifth Century," in *Studies in Numismatic Method Presented to Philip Grierson*, ed. C.N.L. Brooke et al. (Cambridge: Cambridge Univ. Press, 1983), 95-111. The pattern found at Carthage, cited above, is paralleled in Gaul, Italy, and the Balkans.

[20] *Epistola*, 14; *Confessio*, 50. Ed. and trans. by A.B.E. Hood, *St. Patrick: His Writings and Muirchu's Life* (London and Chichester: Phillimore, 1978).

[21] *De Excidio*, 66.3-5. Ed. and trans. by Michael Winterbottom, *Gildas: 'The Ruin of Britain' and Other Works* (London and Chichester: Phillimore, 1978).

[22] *Life of St. John the Almsgiver*, 10. See Dark, *Civitas*, 203; and R.D. Penhallurick, *Tin in Antiquity* (London: Institute of Metals, 1986), 245.

[23] See Esmonde Cleary, *The Ending*, 139; S. Archer, "Late Roman Gold and Silver Coin Hoards in Britain: A Gazetteer," in *The End of Roman Britain*, ed. P.J. Casey, BAR No. 71 (Oxford: BAR Publishing, 1979), 29-64; and Anne S. Robertson, "Romano-British Coin Hoards: Their Numismatic, Archaeological and Historical Significance," in *Coins and the Archaeologist*, 13-37.

[24] Grierson and Mays (17-21) state that the scarcity of gold hoards in Britain "must be due to the province having managed its affairs on a silver rather than on a gold basis," while its neighbors in Gaul did the opposite.

[25] See, for example, Archer, "Late Roman Gold and Silver Coin Hoards in Britain"; Robertson, "Romano-British Coin Hoards"; R.J. Brickstock, *Copies of the Fel Temp Reparatio Coinage in Britain: A Study of Their Chronology and Archaeological Significance Including Gazetteers of Hoards and Site Finds*, BAR British Series No. 176 (Oxford: BAR Publishing, 1987); A.M. Burnett and R.F. Bland, eds., *Coin Hoards from Roman Britain*, vol. 7, British Museum Occasional Paper No. 59 (London: British Museum, 1987); and Blackburn, "Three Silver Coins."

[26] See Robertson, "Romano-British Coin Hoards," 28.

[27] Ibid., 33-34: "[Clusters of] coin hoards to Honorius or later . . . reflect the havoc wrought on life and property by the Saxons [landing on the south and east coasts], by the Scots [along the Severn], and, possibly, by the Picts [on the Yorkshire and Lincolnshire coasts, which] establishes beyond doubt a connection between the widespread loss of treasure and contemporary warfare or other disturbance."

[28] Esmonde Cleary, *The Ending*; Grierson and Mays, 37.

[29] Boon, "Theodosian Coins," 431. Cf. A. Burnett, "Clipped *Siliquae* and the End of Roman Britain," *Britannia* 15 (1984): 163-68 (168): ". . . in Britain alone of the Empire clipping took place on a very extensive scale."

[30] Burnett, "Clipped *Siliquae*." Clipped coins are extremely rare in early fourth-century hoards in Britain, and in these cases the clipping is slight, while in hoards containing coins of 393-411 clipping was rife. Cf. Reece, *Coinage in Roman Britain*, 45: "Andrew Burnett has made the very good point that the clipping of silver coins in Britain belongs to the years up to about 410, and that clipping the coins must be the last phase in their use."

31 Boon, "Theodosian Coins," 431; Grierson and Mays, 37.

32 Kent in Boon, "Theodosian Coins," 431-32. See also Kent, *RIC*, Vol. X, lxxxv: "Clipping may represent the enhanced purchasing power of a *siliqua* as the money-supply dwindled."

33 Grierson and Mays, 39.

34 Esmonde Cleary, *The Ending*, 135.

35 See Grierson and Mays, 18.

36 See Esmonde Cleary, *The Ending*, 139; Grierson and Mays, 15-26 (esp. 17-19). The latter refer to the British silver hoards as "the most astonishing numismatic phenomenon of the late fourth century and the opening decade of the fifth" (18).

37 See map of coin and plate hoards in Esmonde Cleary, *The Ending*, 97.

38 See Grierson and Mays, 20, for relevant publications. The Coleraine hoard contained nearly 1500 *siliquae*, two-thirds of which were clipped. Two coins of Constantine III date the deposition post-407, and c.420 has been suggested, making this Irish raid roughly contemporary with and in the same geographic area as Patrick's captivity.

39 See ibid., 98-99; and Salway, *The Oxford Illustrated History*, 294. Higham (*Rome*, 85) believes that these even weights may suggest diplomatic payments, or the equal rationing out of shared loot.

40 Michael Fulford, "Pottery and Britain's Foreign Trade in the Later Roman Period," in *Pottery and Early Commerce: Characterization and Trade in Roman and Later Ceramics*, ed. D.P.S. Peacock (London/New York/San Francisco: Academic Press, 1977), 35-84. For general discussion of the ceramic industry in late Roman Britain, see Vivien Swan, *The Pottery Kilns of Roman Britain* (London: HMSO, 1984); idem, *Pottery in Roman Britain*, 4th rev. ed. (Aylesbury: Shire Archaeology, 1988); and M.G. Fulford and K. Huddleston, *The Current State of Romano-British Pottery Studies* (London: English Heritage, 1991).

41 Swan, *Pottery in Roman Britain*, 40; Dark, *Discovery*, 93.

42 Henrietta Quinnell, "Cornwall During the Iron Age and Roman Period," *Cornish Archaeology* 25 (1986): 111-34 (129); Swan, *Pottery in Roman Britain*, 40; Dark, *Discovery*, 93.

43 Swan, *Pottery in Roman Britain*, 40.

44 See discussion under Tintagel in the Gazetteer below.

45 See Radford, "Imported Pottery Found at Tintagel, Cornwall," in *Dark Age Britain*, 59-67; and Charles Thomas, "Imported Pottery in Dark-Age Western Britain," *Medieval Archaeology* 3 (1959): 89-111.

46 J.W. Hayes, *Late Roman Pottery* (London: British School at Rome, 1972). See also idem, *A Supplement to Late Roman Pottery* (1980); J. Dore and K. Greene, eds., *Roman Pottery Studies in Britain and Beyond*, BAR Supplemental Series No. 30 (Oxford: BAR Publishing, 1977); and D.P.S. Peacock, *Amphorae and the Roman Economy* (London: Longman, 1986).

47 Charles Thomas, *A Provisional List of Imported Pottery in Post-Roman Western Britain and Ireland* (Redruth: Institute of Cornish Studies, 1981). See also idem, "Imported Late-Roman Mediterranean Pottery in Ireland and Western Britain: Chronologies and Implications," *Proceedings of the Royal Irish Academy* 76C (1976): 245-56; idem, "The Context of Tintagel: a New Model for the Diffusion of Post-Roman Mediterranean Imports," *Cornish Archaeology* 27 (1988): 7-25; and the descriptive catalog of imports in Edwards and Lane, eds., *Early Medieval Settlements in Wales*.

Fig. 1 Distribution of Sites in Sub-Roman Britain: Definite, Probable, and Possible.

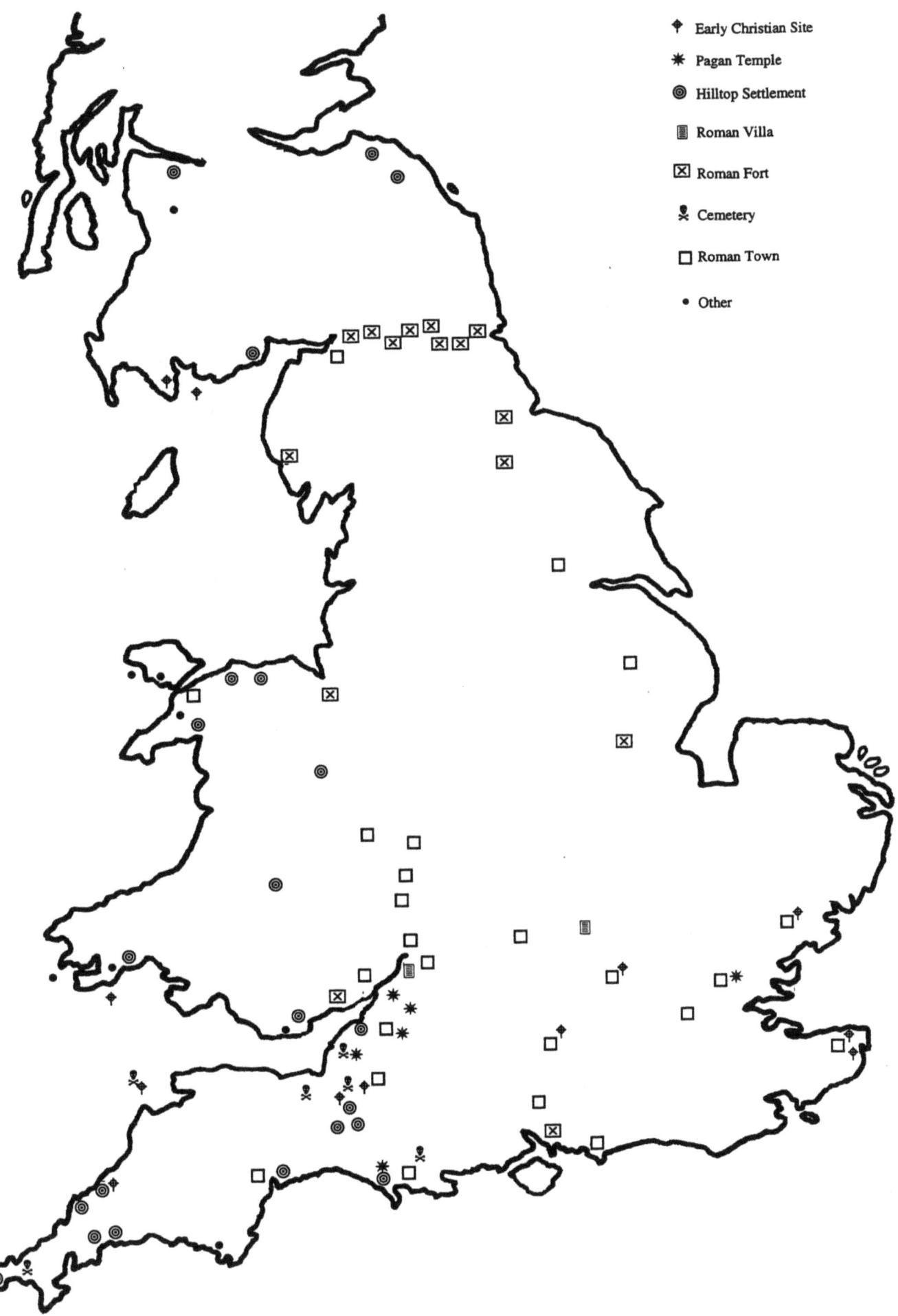

Fig. 2 Distribution of Sites by Type in Late and Sub-Roman Britain.

PART TWO: GAZETTEER OF SITES

The following Gazetteer covers the entire Romanized zone in Britain and "British" settlements extending as far north as the Firth of Forth, and is divided into five regional groupings.[1] Individual sites are listed by their English names (along with Roman and/or Celtic nomenclature, if known) and are ordered alphabetically within their region.

After the name of the site, a designation of "Definite," "Probable," or "Possible" is assigned to each site in accord with the strength of its dating evidence. "Definite" indicates the presence of inhabitable structures associated with one or more examples of the following types of dating evidence: Roman coins (or copies) minted in the fifth or sixth centuries; imported pottery widely recognized as belonging to the fifth or sixth centuries; recent scientifically-tested samples yielding fifth- or sixth-century dates.[2] "Probable" indicates the presence of one or more of the aforementioned evidence types not associated with structures, and/or some evidence of structures associated with one or more of the following: Roman coin issues of the late fourth century; locally-made pottery of the late fourth or fifth centuries; broad-ranging scientific estimates; glass, metalwork, or jewelry datable stylistically to the fifth or sixth centuries. "Possible" indicates the presence of undatable structures or occupation at a late Roman site, stray finds of objects dating to the fifth or sixth centuries, or the testimony of sub-Roman activity in early medieval written sources.

Below the name and rank of the site is a brief description (e.g. hillfort, Roman town, cemetery); a list of datable artefacts or other dating evidence; and a bibliography of excavation reports and commentaries pertaining specifically to that site (general archaeological and historical sources are listed in the Bibliography which follows the Gazetteer). Finally, a brief narrative is included to provide some background to the site, an overview of its evolution, and a sampling of current interpretations.

The East

CANTERBURY (*Durovernum Cantiacorum*)   Definite

Description:
Civitas capital; early Christian site

Dating evidence:
1 coin of Honorius (393-423)
200 coins, "House of Theodosius" issue (388-402)
Christian silver hoard (c.407-11)
1 Gallic *tremissis*, of either Severus III or Zeno (c.480)

Sources:
Bennett, P. "Excavations at 68-69A Stour Street." *Archaeologia Cantiana* 96 (1980): 406-10.
—. "Canterbury." In *The Saxon Shore: A Handbook*, ed. V.A. Maxfield, pp. 118-29. Exeter: Exeter Univ. Press, 1989.
Blockley, P. "Excavations at Ridingate." *Archaeologia Cantiana* 103 (1986): 205-9.
Brooks, D.A. "The Case for Continuity in Fifth-Century Canterbury Re-examined." *Oxford Journal of Archaeology* 7 (1988): 99-114.
Frere, S.S. "Canterbury: The Post-War Excavations." *Archaeologia Cantiana* 100 (1984): 29-46.
Johns, C.M. and Potter, T.W. "The Canterbury Late Roman Treasure." *Antiquaries Journal* 55 (1985): 313-52.
Kent, J.P.C., *et al.* "A Visigothic Gold Tremiss and a Fifth-Century Firesteel from the Marlowe Theatre Site, Canterbury." *Antiquaries Journal* 53 (1983): 371-73.
Sherlock, D. and Woods, H. *St. Augustine's Abbey: Report on Excavations, 1960-78.* Canterbury: Kent Archaeological Society, 1988.

Archaeological fieldwork is revealing many important clues about late Roman Canterbury. While decay and demolition were certainly in evidence in many of Canterbury's public buildings, what is interesting is the re-use of these areas for continued economic activity in the tumultuous fifth century.

The fourth century saw the demolition of the public baths and the portico of the local temple. But the temple courtyard was still being used in the fifth century, perhaps as a market, and new timber structures were built over the baths complex.[3] Although the southern carriageway at Riding Gate was stopped up at this time, its space was maintained for use as a metalworker's workshop.[4] Other fifth-century structures were built over Roman roads, indicating that urban standards may have been declining in Canterbury, but its sub-Roman occupants were choosing adaptation over desertion.

There is other evidence that at least some of these fifth-century occupants were quite wealthy and Christian. An impressive silver hoard was found outside of the London Gate, and is dated from coin evidence to c.407-11 or later.[5] The hoard included silver ingots (late fourth/early fifth century), a gold ring (late fourth), and numerous silver spoons (late fourth) decorated with the *Chi-Rho* monogram. The spoons in particular offer indisputable evidence of a wealthy Christian community in sub-Roman Canterbury that may have provided the precedent for the Augustinian mission of 597.[6]

Other evidence allows us to extend the sub-Roman occupation at least to the end of the fifth century. In the temple precinct archaeologists uncovered a multiple burial, seemingly a family and their pet dog, with associated jewelry dating stylistically to the mid fifth century.[7] Esmonde Cleary points out that this inhumation is in clear violation of the Roman law preventing burial of the dead within town walls.[8] In the Marlowe area, in southeastern Canterbury, excavation revealed timber structures inserted into the shell of an earlier stone building; deposits indicated up to four phases of fifth-century occupation on the site.[9] Nearby, in soil covering a late Roman courtyard, excavators found a Visigothic coin and a firesteel, a metal "match" used to strike flint.[10] The coin, a gold *tremissis* of either Severus III or Zeno, is most likely a Visigothic copy originating in southern Gaul c.480.[11] Its fragmented condition indicates that it was probably part of a goldsmith's collection, as was the firesteel, which is similar to one found at Portchester and dates by affinity to the mid to late fifth century.

CHELMSFORD (*Caesaromagus*)   Probable

Description:
Walled town

Dating Evidence:
Coins of Arcadius
"Jutish" pottery

Sources:
Drury, P.J. "Chelmsford." *Current Archaeology* 41 (1974): 166-76.
Dunnett, Rosalind. *The Trinovantes*. London: Duckworth, 1975.
Rodwell, Warwick and Trevor Rowley, eds. *The 'Small Towns' of Roman Britain*. BAR No. 15. Oxford: BAR Publishing, 1975.

Caesaromagus, "Caesar's Plain," suffered badly from the Boudiccan revolt and could never compete economically with the markets at nearby London and Colchester. The Romans lost interest in developing the small town after the second century, and native Trinovantian influence remained strong in the area.

But in the fourth century, Chelmsford may have taken on a significant religious role. A Romano-Celtic temple was built just outside the city walls c.320 in which, states Drury, "we can see the complete change from the Celtic tradition of worshipping in the open air, to the classical concept of anthropomorphic gods who need houses."[12] The building consists of two concentric octagons, the inner one opening to a semicircular apse on its western wall. "The site," writes Drury, "produced 90 coins more or less equally spread between 310 and 402, ending with issues of Arcadius."[13] Sometime after 402, ritual discontinued at the temple and a small three-room house was erected against its eastern wall. A subsequent fifth-century phase saw the careful demolition of the temple and the removal of its stones, perhaps, as Drury suggests, to build Chelmsford's first Christian church.[14] The small house remained standing, however, and there is evidence that domestic activity continued at the temple site for some time, probably until the late fifth century.[15]

Less is known about Chelmsford's timber structures, traces of which have been found both inside and outside the city walls. One large timber building, destroyed by fire, has been dated to the fifth century because it contained continental pottery identified stylistically as "Jutish." Locally made sub-Roman pottery has also been recorded both at Chelmsford and nearby Great Dunmow. "Presumably," writes Dunnet, "the bulk of the population continued living in their established homes."[16]

CHICHESTER (*Noviomagus Regnorum*)   Probable

Description:
Civitas capital

Dating Evidence:
One bronze coin of Arcadius (c.383-402)
One gold *solidus* of Valentinian III (425-455)

Sources:
Cunliffe, Barry. *The Regni*. London: Duckworth, 1973.
Down, Alec. *Chichester Excavations II-VI*. Chichester: Chichester Civic Society Excavations Committee, 1974-89.
—. *Roman Chichester*. Chichester: Phillimore, 1988.
Down, Alec and John Magilton. *Chichester Excavations VIII*. Chichester: Chichester Civic Society Excavations Committee, 1993.
Down, Alec and Margaret Rule. *Chichester Excavations I*. Chichester: Chichester Civic Society Excavations Committee, 1971.
Welch, M.G. "Late Romans and Saxons in Sussex." *Britannia* 2 (1971): 232-37.
—. *Early Anglo-Saxon Sussex*. BAR No. 112. Oxford: BAR Publishing, 1983.

Chichester shows signs of continued settlement in the fifth century. Its public baths were still functioning in the 370s, and two houses in Chapel Street show signs of occupation into the next century.[17] Fifth-century numismatic evidence includes a bronze coin of Arcadius[18] and a Visigothic copy of a gold *solidus* of Valentinian III.[19] There is also numismatic and ceramic evidence of occupation in the late fourth and early fifth century at some of the neighboring villas and settlements, including Bignor, Rookery Hill, Thundersbarrow, and Bow Hill.[20] Down has speculated that the strongholds of the sub-Roman *tyranni* may have included "the old *civitas* capitals" like Chichester "with their strong walls, the forts of the Saxon shore and, in some instances, the large estates where the owners were sufficiently wealthy to maintain armed forces."[21]

COLCHESTER (*Camulodunum*)   Possible

Description:
Colonia; early Christian site

Dating Evidence:
12 coins dating 388-402 (uncataloged)
Bronze buckle (late fourth century)
Two cruciform brooches

Sources:
Clarke, David T. *Roman Colchester*. Colchester: Colchester Borough Council, 1980.
Crummy, Nina. *Colchester Archaeological Report 5: The Post-Roman Small Finds*. Colchester: Archaeological Trust, 1988.
Crummy, Philip. *Colchester Archaeological Report 1: Aspects of Anglo-Saxon and Norman Colchester*. CBA Research Report No. 39. London: CBA, 1981.
—. *Colchester Archaeological Report 3: Excavations at Lion Walk, Balkerne Lane, and Middleborough*. Colchester: Archaeological Trust, 1984.
—. *In Search of Colchester's Past*. Colchester: Archaeological Trust, 1984.
—. "A Roman Church in Colchester." *Current Archaeology* 120 (1990): 406-8.
Dunnet, Rosalind. *The Trinovantes*. London: Duckworth, 1975.

Colchester, Roman Britain's first capital and *colonia*, was on its way to becoming the model provincial city before its destruction by Boudicca in AD 61. Though rebuilt, Colchester was once again vulnerable to the attacks of seaborne raiders in the fourth and fifth centuries. Excavations at Duncan's Gate and Balkerne Lane have revealed evidence of fire-destruction and external attacks in the fourth century.[22]

Coin finds and graves testify to continuous occupation into the early years of the fifth century.[23] Other fifth-century evidence includes one sunken-floored hut, two cruciform brooches, and parts of military belt-buckles.[24] The military buckles could have belonged to any late Roman soldier, but the fact that the hut and graves were found within Colchester's walls suggests that these occupants were present at a time when the Roman restriction against intra-mural burials no longer existed.[25] The area around the Balkerne Gate, which remains to this day largely intact, may yet yield clues about sub-Roman defense and transportation.

Recent excavations at one Roman cemetery near the present-day Police Station revealed startling evidence of a substantial Christian community in late Roman Colchester.[26] A small pagan cemetery was apparently succeeded by a larger Christian cemetery in the early fourth century. Most of the bodies were in nailed wooden coffins, though some were in lead coffins, hollowed tree trunks, timber vaults, or no coffins at all. To one side of this cemetery excavators found the circuit of a long rectangular stone building, with timber inner partitions, oriented east-west. It seems to have been constructed between 320-40, with later alterations including a rounded apse added at the eastern end. The structural design strongly suggests that this building was a Christian church, though no Christian artifacts have yet been found. The interior did yield, however, hundreds of fourth-century coins, five complete oil lamps, an iron frying pan, and bird and pig bones. The excavator suggests that the latter may have been part of a funerary or other ritual meal.[27]

LONDON (*Londinium Augusta*)   Definite

Description:
Provincial/diocesan capital; seaport

Dating Evidence:
2 "chip-carved" bronze buckles
200+ Theodosian bronze coins (c.388-402)
Gold and silver issues of Arcadius and Honorius
One silver ingot (c.405)
Imported pottery (Biv, Bv, and Bvi)

Sources:
Chapman, Hugh. "London," in *The Saxon Shore: A Handbook*, ed. Valerie A. Maxfield, pp. 113-17. Exeter: Exeter Univ. Press, 1989.
Hall, Jenny and Ralph Merrifield. *Roman London*. London: HMSO, 1986.
Hill, Charles, Martin Millet, and Thomas Blagg. *The Roman Wall and Monumental Arch in London*. Special Paper No. 3. London: London and Middlesex Archaeological Society, 1980.
Hobley, Brian. *Roman and Saxon London*. London: Museum of London, 1985. This work includes a comprehensive bibliography of London excavation reports.
Marsden, Peter. *Roman London*. London: Thames and Hudson, 1980.
—. "London in the Third and Fourth centuries," in *Roman Urban Topography in Britain and the Western Empire*, ed. Francis Grew and Brian Hobley, pp. 99-108. CBA Report No. 59. London: CBA, 1985.
Merrifield, Ralph. *London, City of the Romans*. London: Batsford, 1983.
Milne, Gustav. *The Port of Roman London*. London: Batsford, 1985.
—. *From Roman Basilica to Medieval Market*. London: HMSO, 1992.
Morris, John. *Londinium: London in the Roman Empire*. Rev. by Sarah Macready. London: Weidenfeld and Nicolson, 1982.
Painter, K.S. *A Roman Silver Ingot*. British Museum Occasional Paper No. 35. London: Dept. of Greek and Roman Antiquities, Acquisitions 1976, 1981.
Palmer, Susann. *Excavation of the Roman and Saxon Site at Orpington*. London: Borough of Bromley, 1984.
Perring, Dominic. *Roman London*. London: Seaby, 1991.
Philp, Brian. "The Forum of Roman London." *Britannia* 9 (1977): 1-64.
Vince, Alan. *Saxon London*. London: Seaby, 1990.

Settlement continued in London into the fifth and sixth centuries, but its character changed dramatically from its once-lofty status as an administrative center of the province. The great basilica was carefully demolished at the start of the fourth century; its apse was left standing and became part of some new structure standing alone on the now-vacant forum.[28]

The London waterfront, on the other hand, showed signs of revival in the late fourth century.[29] Urban occupation continued there until the sixth century, and there is some evidence—a brooch and *amphorae*—of continued trade with the Continent.[30] A section of the riverside wall was rebuilt at this time, while towers were added (c.350) to the landward wall.[31] These defensive measures fit in with late fourth-century imperial policy and are paralleled at other walled cities in Britain.

The *Notitia Dignitatum* states that London housed the imperial treasury (and its overseer, the *praepositus Thesaurorum Augustensium*) in the last decade of the fourth century. A silver ingot, of the type presented to the army on an imperial accession or anniversary, was found within the Tower of London in a hoard that also contained a silver coin of Arcadius and two gold coins, one of Honorius and one of Arcadius.[32] Scattered around the Tower as well were several coins running down to 388-402, leading Perring to postulate that a late Roman salient was built on the Tower site in the last decades of the fourth century, perhaps associated with the campaigns of Stilicho.[33]

But the site which gives the clearest evidence of fifth-century occupation is a masonry building uncovered in Lower Thames Street near Billingsgate.[34] This large house had under-floor heating and a private bath-suite, all of which continued to be used well into the fifth century. A hoard of over two hundred copper coins issued between 388 and 402 were found scattered on the furnace room floor,[35] and under the furnace ashes was found a piece of fifth-century amphora imported from the eastern Mediterranean, probably Gaza. The *terminus* of this occupation is marked by broken glass and roof debris, on which was found a circular brooch identical to one found in an early (pagan) Saxon grave at Mitcham, Surrey.

There is little evidence of "Germanic" pottery or *Grubenhäuser* in the city itself,[36] though a "Saxon" cemetery has been identified in the London suburb of Orpington.[37] Anglo-Saxon London (*Lundenwic*) grew up to the west of the city and did not become a significant *burg* until quite late. In fact, the *Anglo-Saxon Chronicle* describes London as a place to which the **Britons** fled after defeat in Kent in the 450s.[38] Perring sees London as the center of a minor sub-Roman kingdom surrounded by banked ditches, constructed to mark the boundaries between it and the sub-Roman communities of Verulamium and Canterbury.[39] The Roman fort at Cripplegate may have passed from the control of these sub-Roman Britons to become an Anglo-Saxon royal palace.[40] But the archaeological evidence is not yet able to clear up all of the questions posed by London. Ironically, Roman Britain's largest city appears not to have been a significant settlement in the immediate post-Roman years, though finds definitely show sporadic activity in the fifth century.

PORTCHESTER (*Portus Adurni*)   Possible

Description:
Saxon Shore fort

Sources:
Cunliffe, Barry. *The Regni*. London: Duckworth, 1973.
—. *Excavations at Portchester Castle, Vol. I: Roman*. Society of Antiquaries Research Report No. 32. London: Society of Antiqaries, 1975.
—. *Excavations at Portchester Castle, Vol. II: Saxon*. Society of Antiquaries Research Report No. 33. London: Society of Antiquaries, 1976.
Munby, Julian. "Portchester." In *The Saxon Shore: A Handbook*, ed. Valerie A. Maxfield, pp. 160-62. Exeter: Exeter Univ. Press, 1989.

A civilian population grew alongside the military presence in the Saxon Shore fort of Portchester. Occupation within the walls was intensive in the fourth century and continued at least into the early fifth century.[41] It is not yet clear whether this fifth-century occupation was the continuation of the military community or a new settlement.[42] Cunliffe's excavations in the 1960s and 70s revealed what he considered a strong "Germanic" presence at Portchester. Continental pottery, Frankish jewelry, and *Grubenhäuser* were found alongside the Roman finds inside the walls of the fort.[43] Cunliffe interpreted these as clear signs of a settled Germanic detachment (*laeti*?) who maintained some contacts with the Continent and shared space inside the fort with the sub-Roman Britons.[44]

RICHBOROUGH (*Rutupiae*)   Probable

Description:
Saxon Shore fort; early Christian site

Dating Evidence:
13,000 bronze coins ("uncertain Theodosian")
4,200 bronze coins of Arcadius
1,000 bronze coins of Honorius
1 gold *tremissis* of Leo I (Italian mint, c.461-74)

Sources:
Blagg, T.F.C. "Richborough." In *The Saxon Shore: A Handbook*, ed. Valerie A. Maxfield, pp. 140-45. Exeter: Exeter Univ. Press, 1989.
Brown, P.D.C. "The Church at Richborough." *Britannia* 2 (1971): 225.
Cunliffe, B.W. *Fifth Report on the Excavations of the Roman Fort at Richborough*. Soc. of Antiquaries Research Report No. 23. London: Soc. of Antiquaries, 1968.
Johnson, Stephen E. "The Construction of the Saxon Shore Fort at Richborough." In *Collectanea Historica: Essays in Memory of Stuart Rigold*, ed. A. Detsicas, pp. 23-31. Maidstone: Kent Archaeological Society, 1981.
Welsby, Derek A. *The Roman Military Defense of the British Provinces in its Later Phases*. BAR British Series No. 101. Oxford: BAR Publishing, 1982.

Rutupiae, "muddy waters," was once one of Roman Britain's main south coast ports, welcoming such visitors as Claudius and Count Theodosius. Though it once guarded the southern approach to the Wantsum Channel, which separated the Isle of Thanet from the rest of Kent, changing water levels have now left it some 4 km from the sea. Excavations in the early part of this century uncovered an exceptionally numerous quantity of Roman coins of the House of Theodosius, which account for 45% of all coinage found within the fort.[45] The coins, along with other late Roman military metalwork recovered, indicate that Richborough was one of the last places in Roman Britain to have been held in full military strength.[46]

By the early fifth century a Christian community was established within the (abandoned?) fort of Richborough. The foundations of a hexagonal masonry structure identified as a baptismal font were uncovered inside the fort, in the north-west corner, along with artifacts bearing the *Chi-Rho* monogram.[47]

Johnson sees the Richborough evidence as fitting in with the pattern repeated in other parts of the late Empire, "where bishops were glad to establish their congregations within the safety of the now abandoned fort walls."[48]

ST. ALBANS (*Verlamion, Verulamium*) Definite

Description:
Municipia; early Christian site

Dating Evidence:
14 (?) bronze coins of Arcadius
3 (?) bronze coins of Eugenius (392-4)
1 silver coin of Honorius, from Milan (397-404)
2 bronze coins of Honorius
36 (?) "House of Theodosius" issue coins
252 sherds of Romano-British pottery (late fifth century)
Imported pottery (1 sherd from a Mediterranean amphora)
Silver hand-pin (sixth or seventh century)

Sources:
Biddle, Martin and Birthe Kjølbye-Biddle. *The Origins of Saint Albans Abbey: Excavations in the Cloister 1982-83*. St. Albans: Abbey Research Committee, 1984.
Branigan, Keith. *Town and Country: The Archaeology of Verulamium and the Roman Chilterns*. Bourne End, Buckinghamshire: Spurbooks, 1973.
—. *The Catuvellauni*. Gloucester: Sutton, 1985.
Frere, Sheppard. *Verulamium Excavations (1972-84)*. Vols. 1-3. London: Society of Antiquaries, 1983.
Niblett, Rosalind. "Verulamium Since the Wheelers." In *Roman Towns: The Wheeler Inheritance: A Review of 50 Years' Research*, ed. Stephen J. Greep, pp. 78-92. CBA Research Report No. 93. York: CBA, 1993.
Selkirk, Andrew and Rosalind Niblett. "Verulamium." *Current Archaeology* 120 (1990): 410-17.

Verulamium is one of the strongest cases for the survival of a major Roman town into the fifth and sixth centuries. Frere's excavations in the 1970s and 80s of Verulamium Insula XXVII reveal a diversity of both public and private activity during the sub-Roman period. One townhouse alone in Insula XXVII reveals the complexity of this activity.[49] Built c.380 on a vacant site, the house included 22 ground-floor rooms and a colonnade surrounding a garden or courtyard. After a period of use, two extensions were added to the house, complete with a series of high-quality mosaic floors whose replacement was necessitated by constant wear. The kitchen floor alone was re-paved four times between about 400 and 430, when a hole was cut through it for the placement of a corn-drying oven or small hypocaust. The oven was used so much that it too needed repairs before the house was demolished c.460. At this stage a large rectangular structure, interpreted as a stone barn or hall, was constructed on the site. After another undetermined period of use, one of the stone buttresses of this building was damaged by the laying of a wooden water pipe, constructed—in the Roman style—with hollowed-out trunks joined by iron collars. Dating is based on associated coins and pottery—of the first decade of the fifth century—and on the continuing stratigraphic sequence which, the excavator estimates, ran down to 475+.

Branigan notes that the construction of the sub-Roman water main indicates that 1) Roman hydraulic engineering skills were still alive in Britain; 2) the Roman aqueduct which served Verulamium was still functioning; and 3) municipal authorities were still working for the maintenance of the city c.450-70.[50] The quality mosaic pavements, found in several houses, would seem to indicate that the skills of the mosaicist were also still alive in fifth-century Britain.

There are further reasons to be as optimistic about the agrarian economy of Verulamium and its environs. The forum, with its well-worn floor, survived into the fifth century. Branigan takes this as an indicator of the continued occupation of the surrounding villa estates, which needed such markets for their goods.[51] Two cottages in Gadebridge Park were occupied at least into the early fifth century, when animal pens were built as additions.[52] There is also slight evidence that Verulamium benefited from Mediterranean trade in the sub-Roman period. The floor of a timber building in Insula XIX was terraced into a previously open cobbled area at some time after 388, and lying on its surface was a quantity of late Roman material, including a pin, brooches, and sherd of an amphora imported from the eastern Mediterranean.[53] "The current picture of late Roman *Verulamium* is one of widespread occupation," comments Rosalind Niblett, "increasingly in timber buildings, amidst areas of open cultivated land; ... but the standard of living was not necessarily low, witness the new water pipe and the imported amphora."[54]

This survival of a Verulamium community in the fifth century has also been inferred from Constantius's *Life of St. Germanus*, which describes Germanus's visit to the shrine of St. Alban in 429. Many scholars have argued for the survival of a "British" population into the sixth century in what has been described as a Saxon-free "Chiltern Zone."[55] According to the *Anglo-Saxon Chronicle*, the area remained in the hands of the Britons until their defeat at the Battle of Bedcanford in 571.[56] When King Offa of Mercia founded St. Albans Abbey in 793, it is likely that he chose a site with previous Christian activity. Excavations at the Abbey, which lies just outside of Verulamium, have revealed evidence of near-continuous activity from the late Roman period to the Dissolution of the Monasteries in the sixteenth century. The earliest level, below the Norman *cellarium* and Anglo-Saxon church, contained several pits, iron nails, charcoal and cremated bones, a silver hand-pin, Roman tile and glass, 32 Roman coins (all but one or two of fourth-century date), and 252 sherds of Romano-British pottery.[57]

Although there is no conclusive evidence for an early Christian cemetery which might have contained the martyred Alban's remains, the finds suggest "intensive use of the site during the growth of [Alban's] cult in the fourth and fifth centuries."[58] The silver pin is of "Celtic" type and dates by affinity to the sixth or seventh century, while the pottery—"grass- or chaff-tempered"—is of late fifth- or sixth-century date.[59] Seventh-century "Saxon" material, together with a reference to St. Alban's shrine in Bede, would suggest that there was some continuity of occupation, perhaps a mixture of pagan and Christian,[60] from the fifth century to the foundation of the Anglo-Saxon Abbey by Offa.

The Southwest

BANTHAM   Probable

Description:
Temporary dune settlement

Dating Evidence:
Roman fine wares
Imported pottery (Bi, Bii, and E ware)
One enamelled disc brooch (Roman)
Two penannular brooches (sub-Roman)
Six iron knife blades

Sources:

Fox, Aileen. "Some Evidence for a Dark Age Trading Site at Bantham, Near Thurlestone, South Devon." *Antiquaries Journal* 35 (1955): 55-67.

Jenkins, H.L. "Ancient Camp at the Mouth of the River Avon." *Devon Cornwall Notes Queries* 2 (1902): 20-23.

Silvester, R.J. "An Excavation on the Post-Roman Site at Bantham, South Devon." *Proceedings of the Devon Archaeological Society* 39 (1981): 89-118.

Bantham Ham at the mouth of the River Avon has, since the eighteenth century, been known to locals as a repository of ancient garbage. Several middens were uncovered by farmers in the nineteenth century, and many of the objects found were collected in 1902 by H.L. Jenkins.[61] In 1953 Aileen Fox identified some of the ceramic finds as sherds of imported pottery dating to the fifth to seventh centuries.[62] A sub-Roman date was then ascribed to this Devon dunes settlement.

Small-scale excavations at the dunes in April 1978 revealed more midden material overlying hearths and adjacent hollows, defined by the excavator as Areas A, B, C, and D.[63] Area A contained a hearth, stake-holes (thought to represent tent-supports), a shallow gully, charcoal pipes, shells, slate slabs, animal bones, a knife blade and other iron fragments, part of an enamelled brooch, and several sherds of pottery (two of which had been pierced to make whorls). Area B was similarly rich, producing several pits, limpet shells, slate slabs, bone fragments, two hearths, charcoal, 70 stake-holes, whetstones, several iron objects, and a single sherd of imported pottery (E ware). Area C yielded only bone and shell fragments, charcoal, and mussel shells, while Area D contained charcoal deposits, several slate slabs, a group of five stake-holes, mussel and limpet shells, and a decorated bone comb.

Analysis of the pottery (21 sherds were found in the most recent excavation) by the excavator identified Roman fine wares and more examples of the imported pottery identified by Fox, the latter representing Mediterranean amphoras (Bi and Bii) and Gaulish kitchenware (E ware).[64] Sixty-one iron objects and fragments were uncovered, including a nail, chisel, clamps, and six knife blades (probably once adorned with wooden shafts). Finely crafted objects found at the site included fragments of a decorated bone comb, two penannular brooches (one bronze and one iron), and a leaded bronze enamelled disc brooch. The penannular brooches have been identified as sub- or post-Roman, while the disc brooch is likely of Roman provincial manufacture (second or third century).[65] Finally, a great quantity of marine shells and animal bones were uncovered, the latter representing (in decreasing order) cattle, sheep, goat, pig, dog, horse, deer, hare, vole, birds, and fish.

The large number of artifacts and slight evidence of structures has led observers to conclude that Bantham was a temporarily, perhaps seasonally, occupied settlement.[66] A sub-Roman trading post, with occasional but intense use, seems likely because of the location and the Mediterranean imports. The iron fragments, along with a single find of iron slag and eleven whorls, suggest that manufacturing may have occured along side, or in relationship to, the long distance trade.

BATH (*Aquae Sulis*)   Probable

Description:
Pagan shrine; small town; spa complex

Dating Evidence:
One hoard of *siliquae*, with coins dating from c.347-88
42 coins, "House of Theodosius" issue (388-402)
Late fourth-century pottery
Imported pottery (Biv)
Organically-tempered pottery (c.450-900)
Penannular brooch

Sources:

Cunliffe, Barry. *Roman Bath Discovered*. London: Routledge and Kegan Paul, 1971; rev. ed., 1984.

—. "The Excavations of the Roman Spring at Bath, 1979." *Antiquaries Journal* 60 (1980): 187-206.

—. *The City of Bath*. Gloucester: Sutton, 1986.

Cunliffe, Barry, ed. *Excavations in Bath, 1950-1975*. Excavation Report No. 1. Bristol: Committee for Rescue Archaeology in Avon, Gloucestershire and Somerset, 1979.

—. *The Temple of Sulis Minerva at Bath: Vol. 2, The Finds from the Sacred Spring*. Oxford: Oxford Univ. Committee for Archaeology, 1988.

Cunliffe, Barry and Davenport, Peter. *The Temple of Sulis Minerva at Bath: Vol. 1, The Site*. Oxford: Oxford Univ. Committee for Archaeology, 1985.

Davenport, Peter, ed. *Archaeology in Bath 1976-1985*. Oxford Univ. Committee for Archaeology Monograph 28. Oxford: Oxford Univ. Comittee for Archaeology, 1991.

O'Leary, T.J. "Excavations at Upper Borough Walls, Bath, 1980." *Medieval Archaeology* 25 (1981): 1-30.

After a defensive wall was built around the religious precinct of Bath in the early fourth century, more and more people began abandoning their extra-mural settlements and moving inside the walled "city." At least 11 major buildings, some quite large and several with underfloor heating and mosaics, makes Bath the most thriving of the small towns in late Roman Britain.[67] A recently found hoard of silver coins shows that the wealth spread to the surrounding communities as well.[68]

The flourishing baths complex underwent dramatic changes at the end of the fourth century. The increasing problem of flooding shut down the underfloor heating for long periods, though the numbers of people visiting the springs did not decrease. The precinct of the Temple of Sulis Minerva saw the most drastic changes, perhaps as the result of the rising influence of Christianity in the area.[69] The Temple altar was dismantled and sculpted blocks were torn from the "Gorgon" pediment, then overturned and used to pave the floors. The colonnade in the outer precinct was demolished and new secular buildings were constructed in its place.

The most complex and significant sequence occurred in the temple's inner paved precinct.[70] The paved floor had been swept regularly until the middle of the fourth century, when an accumulation of earth began to cover it (and a coin of Constans, c.347-48). A new cobbled floor was then laid on top of the dirt, and again dirt began to accumulate over the worn stones. This pattern was repeated six times until the final collapse of the buildings sealed the sequence with a blanket of masonry rubble. The third level of cobbling sealed a "House of Theodosius" coin (388-402) and related pottery (Oxford color-coated ware and shell-tempered ware), but that leaves three layers of pavement, each of them worn by the passage of feet, extending to a time beyond the last coin issues and datable pottery.

The excavators believe that the chronology of this sequence extends occupation of the temple precinct at least to 470, and very likely into the sixth century and beyond.[71] While the pottery experts would like to compress the entire chronology into the late fourth century (squeezing the last three layers into the 390s), most archaeologists agree with Cunliffe (and the coin evidence from here and the sacred spring) that settlement must extend well into the fifth century.[72]

Evidence elsewhere supports the theory that Bath remained populated through the sub-Roman period. Throughout the baths complex the floor slabs, especially beneath the doorways, showed considerable wear in the last (fifth-century) phase, indicating that "even though the buildings were now being demolished, the spring continued to be frequented on an impressive scale."[73] While there was much stone-robbing in the post-Roman years, not all the buildings were demolished. The reservoir enclosure survived into the early medieval period and became known as the King's Bath.[74] "Elsewhere within the walled area" of Bath, writes Cunliffe, "there are hints of domestic buildings being used well into the fifth and possibly the sixth centuries."[75] Such "hints" include the Abbeygate Street site, where a Roman building that had collapsed in the late fourth century was replaced, after an interval, by a new structure erected on a different alignment, the associated stratigraphy arguing for survival well beyond 410. Excavation has thus lent some credence to the assertion of the *Anglo-Saxon Chronicle* that, at the time of the Battle of Dyrham (c.577), Bath was a major *civitas* and (perhaps) the residence of a British king.[76]

BREAN DOWN   Probable

Description:
Cemetery; religious shrine/church

Dating Evidence:
Three coins of Constantine II (c.330-7)
Theodosian coinage (down to 395)
Radiocarbon estimates of three skeletons (calibrated: 415-600; 560-660; 654-786)

Sources:
Ap Simon, A.M. "The Roman Temple on Brean Down, Somerset." *Proceedings of the University of Bristol Spelaeological Society* 10 (1964-65): 195-258.
Bell, M. *Brean Down Excavations 1983-87*. London: English Heritage, 1990.

Excavation has revealed what has been identified as a sub-Roman cemetery at Brean Down. Three skeletons yielded calibrated radiocarbon dates of 415-600, 560-660, and 654-786. The skeletons were aligned east-west but were not buried with grave-goods. Nearby stones suggest a return to the pre-Roman trait of slab-lined and cist burials.[77] The east-west alignment and lack of grave-goods have been interpreted as Christian burials. A Romano-Celtic temple was built on the Down c.340 and demolished c.390.[78] This was replaced by a small, rectangular, stone-built structure. One interpretation is that the pagan temple was demolished by the Christian community, who replaced it with a small shrine.[79] But the rectangular structure could have been a subsequent pagan shrine, abandoned sometime after the coming of the Christians.[80]

CADBURY-CONGRESBURY   Definite

Description:
Hillfort

Dating Evidence:
Bronze penannular brooch
Romano-British pottery (538 sherds, representing a minimum of 170 vessels)
Imported pottery (PRSW, ARSW, B *amphorae*, and D ware)
Anglo-Saxon glass and ceramics

Sources:
Burrow, Ian. *Hillfort and Hill-Top Settlement in Somerset in the First to Eighth Centuries AD*. BAR British Series No. 91. Oxford: BAR Publishing, 1981.
—. "Roman Material from Hillforts." In *The End of Roman Britain*, ed. P.J. Casey, pp. 212-29. BAR No. 71. Oxford: BAR Publishing, 1979.
Fowler, P.J. *et al. Cadbury Congresbury, Somerset, 1968: An Introductory Report*. Bristol: Univ. of Bristol Dept. of Extra-Mural Studies, 1970.

Rahtz, Philip and P.J. Fowler. "Somerset AD 400-700." In *Archaeology and the Landscape*, ed. P.J. Fowler, pp. 187-221. London: J. Baker, 1972.

Rahtz, Philip, et al. *Cadbury Congresbury 1968-73: A Late/Post-Roman Hilltop Settlement in Somerset*. BAR British Series No. 223. Oxford: BAR Publishing, 1992.

Cadbury-Congresbury (Cadcong) is an Iron Age hillfort that was reoccupied in the late or post-Roman period. Around AD 400 new earthworks were constructed, including a bank dividing the hillfort into two parts and a linking entrance way.[81] These earthworks included both late Romano-British pottery and fifth- and sixth-century pottery imported from the Mediterranean, putting the reoccupation of Cadcong within the timeframe 400-700.[82]

According to its excavators, Cadcong's defensive rampart "is not a major military work, with extensive use of timberframing or revetment (as at South Cadbury); but rather a flat platform on which turf or a light superstructure was piled."[83] However, traces of other defensive structures found at Cadcong, including bastions and watchtowers, argue for a more intensive fortified use. Burrow estimates the manpower needed to defend Cadcong and its inhabitants as between 400 and 650 men.[84]

But Cadcong's defenses are only part of the story. Several domestic buildings were discerned from excavation, as well as a gatehouse and a roundhouse identified by the excavators as a possible shrine or temple.[85] Evidence of metalworking is abundant at Cadcong, which is also one of the sites which has yielded the largest amount of imported Mediterranean *amphorae*.[86] By the sixth century, the residents of Cadcong had attained, in the opinion of the excavators, "high status, patronising craft-workers and having access to glass and ceramics from the Anglo-Saxon areas to the East, and from the Eastern Mediterannean."[87]

Still, there is much debate over the exact function of this hilltop settlement. Some of the possibilities are:

1) A regional "fair" or marketplace, perhaps occupied only seasonally.[88]

2) A court hosting an itinerant "over-king."[89]

3) A monastic enclosure (St. Congar's monastery).[90]

There is no conclusive evidence for any of these possiblities. Until we have a better understanding of the reoccupation of hillforts in general, Cadcong is best left as a "high-status" site.[91]

There may be other contextual clues, however, if we look at sub-Roman Somerset. Fowler believes that the inhabitants of Cadcong came from nearby Gatcombe, a walled villa and late Roman community.[92] This would parallel what Alcock has suggested for South Cadbury hillfort, that its sub-Roman inhabitants had migrated from nearby Ilchester (*Lindinis*).[93] Cadcong lies at the junction of three tribal kingdoms: the Dobunni, the Durotriges, and the Dumnonii. Given the intensive sub-Roman occupation of hillforts and other settlements in this area, these Britons may have been responsible for the construction of Wansdyke as a defensive border between their *civitates* and the encroaching Saxons.[94] The inhabitants of Cadcong seem to have enjoyed undisturbed peace until the late sixth or early seventh century, when the settlement declined and was abandoned.[95]

CANNINGTON   Probable

Description:
Hillfort; religious shrine; cemetery

Dating Evidence:
Carbon 14 determinations
Bronze penannular brooch
Imported pottery (Bii and Bmisc)

Sources:
Hanley, Robin. *Villages in Roman Britain*. Aylesbury: Shire Archaeology, 1987.

Rahtz, P.A. "Late Roman Cemeteries and Beyond." In *Burial in the Roman World*, ed. R. Reece, pp. 53-64. CBA Research Report No. 2. London: CBA, 1977.

Rahtz, P.A. and Watts, L., "The End of Roman Temples in the West of Britain." In *The End of Roman Britain*, ed. P.J. Casey, pp. 183-201. BAR No. 71. Oxford: BAR Publishing, 1979.

Cannington, in Somerset, is the site of one of the largest Roman cemeteries excavated in Britain. The cemetery originally consisted of some 2000-5000 graves—only 500 of which survived to be excavated—and was in use from the second century to the seventh or eighth. The earlier graves were aligned roughly north-south and contained grave-goods, while the latter were aligned east-west and lacked grave-goods, suggesting an initially pagan and subsequently Christianized community.

Two explanations have been offered for the size and location of the cemetery. One scenario is that the local Romano-British population migrated to the nearby hillfort and used Cannington as their burial-ground.[96] This is likely to have happened in the sub-Roman period, but does not explain the second-century graves, for the hillfort reoccupation is unlikely to have been that early. (Though a late Roman temple, found on the hilltop, could account for some of the early pagan graves.[97]) Another explanation is that Cannington served as a communal burial ground for several communities in Somerset, as was probably the case for Poundbury near Dorchester.[98]

CASTLE DORE   Possible

Description:
Hillfort

Dating Evidence:
Imported pottery (1 vessel, unidentified)
Glass beads

Sources:
Quinnell, H. and D. Haris. "Castle Dore: the Chronology Reconsidered." *Cornish Archaeology* 24 (1985): 123-32.

Radford, C.A. Ralegh. "Romance and Reality in Cornwall: Castle Dore." In *The Quest for Arthur's Britain*, ed. Geoffrey Ashe, pp. 70-77. New York: Paladin, 1971.

Radford, C.A. Ralegh and Michael J. Swanton. *Arthurian Sites in the West*. Exeter: Exeter Univ. Press, 1975.

Rahtz, Philip. "Castle Dore—A Reappraisal of the Post-Roman Structures." *Cornish Archaeology* 10 (1971): 49-54.

Castle Dore is an artificial earthwork created in the pre-Roman Iron Age. It consists of a circular plateau surrounded by two concentric banks, about eight feet high, and two deep ditches. Radford's excavations in the 1930s identified Castle Dore as a hillfort reoccupied and refortified at the end of the Roman period, in use through the fifth, sixth, and seventh centuries.

Few traces of the fortifications were discovered. A dry stone revetment was added to the old earthen banks to make a fighting platform, and a small oval hut just inside the gateway was likely used as a guardhouse.[99] From the gateway a rough cobbled road, about six feet wide, led to the interior plateau and past several wooden structures. From posthole patterns, Radford identified these structures as two large halls (90 ft. x 40 ft. and 65 ft. x 35 ft.) and two granaries (7 ft. x 5 ft.). Though some archaeologists have questioned Radford's interpretation of these features,[100] Rahtz maintains that "the post-Roman complex at Castle Dore remains . . . the most impressive 'palace' in the west."[101]

Dating evidence is scarce at Castle Dore. Those structures labeled sub-Roman clearly overlay Iron Age features, but only a few beads and pottery sherds were found in the sub-Roman layer. The sherds are from one vessel of imported pottery, of unidentifiable type but similar to a grey vessel (sixth century) found at Gwithian.[102] D.F. Williams, however, believes the sherds to be from *amphorae* of the pre-conquest period.[103] Castle Dore's proximity to the "Tristan stone" (DRUSTANUS HIC IACIT / CUNOMORI FILIUS) has led to the belief that this fort was the residence of Cunomorus (King Mark), a sixth-century prince named in a Dumnonian genealogy.

CHUN CASTLE   Probable

Description:
Hillfort

Dating Evidence:
Grass-marked pottery
Imported amphora (Bi)
Metalworking debris

Source:
Thomas, Charles. "Evidence for Post-Roman Occupation of Chun Castle, Cornwall." *Antiquaries Journal* 36 (1956): 75-78.

Chun Castle is a bivallate walled enclosure occupied in both the Roman and sub-Roman periods. Excavations revealed dry stone structures, a hearth associated with grass-marked pottery, fragments from one vessel of Aegean origin (mid sixth century), a crude furnace, and a block of smelted tin.[104]

DORCHESTER (*Durnovaria*)/POUNDBURY   Definite

Description:
Civitas capital and cemetery

Dating Evidence:
Theodosian bronze coins (c.388-402)
One silver hoard, ending with issues of Honorius
Six radiocarbon estimates (fourth to seventh centuries)
Organically-tempered pottery (late fifth or sixth century)
Imported pottery (Biv and Bv)

Sources:
Draper, Jo and Christopher Chaplin. *Dorchester Excavations Vol. 1*. Dorchester: Dorset Natural History and Archaeological Society, 1982.

Farwell, D.E. and T.L. Molleson. *Excavations at Poundbury 1966-1980. Vol. II: The Cemeteries*. Dorset Natural History and Archaeological Society Monograph No. 11. Dorchester: Dorset Natural History and Archaeological Society, 1993.

Green, C.J.S. "The Cemetery of a Romano-British Community at Poundbury, Dorchester, Dorset." In *The Early Church in Western Britain and Ireland*, ed. S. Pearce, pp. 61-76. BAR British Series No. 102. Oxford: BAR Publishing, 1982.

—. *Excavations at Poundbury, Dorchester, Dorset 1966-1982. Vol. I: The Settlements*. Dorset Natural History and Archaeological Society Monograph No. 7. Dorchester: Dorset Natural History and Archaeological Society, 1988.

Late Roman Dorchester produced one of Britain's most distinctive schools for mosaicists and was the home of a flourishing Christian community. Over a thousand graves have been examined at nearby Poundbury, one of three major Christian cemeteries identified in Roman Britain.[105] The majority of the graves were aligned east-west and were in simple wooden coffins without grave goods, though others were in more elaborate stone or lead coffins and included a few grave goods. Within some of the coffins at the "main cemetery," bodies were partially preserved by a packing of gypsum plaster.[106] A coin pendant with the *Chi-Rho*, along with the east-west alignments (which carefully avoid earlier north-south inhumations), strongly suggest that many of these were Christian graves.

The Dorchester area has yielded other evidence of early Christians. The villas at Frampton and Hinton St. Mary both contained mosaics bearing such Christian symbols as the *Chi-Rho*, and presumably these mosaics were part of private chapels. These and stone mausolea found in the Christian section at Poundbury suggest that Christianity was spreading among the upper classes in the fourth century. By c.420, however, the cemetery went out of use, and a substantial agricultural community grew up on the site (the enclosed area equals that of South Cadbury). Features of this post-Roman settlement include fifteen buildings (post-built, beam-slot, combined post-and-beam, and sunken-featured structures), seven groups of pits, six grain driers and a threshing floor, four small ditched enclosures, and a substantial ditched enclosure.[107] Additionally, six mausolea belonging to the late Roman cemetery were either robbed or re-used in the post-Roman period, one yielding a Theodosian bronze coin sealed in its wall plaster.[108] This settlement seems to have had two phases, spanning (on radiocarbon estimates) from the late fourth to early seventh centuries. Sherds of imported *amphorae*, quality iron knives, and bone pins tell us something of Poundbury's economic and industrial activities, while the large number of grain driers might suggest on-site mass processing of grain.[109] The end of sub-Roman Poundbury was sudden, marked by the destruction of drystone and timber structures and the possible slaughter of animals, with radiocrabon estimates suggesting a date in the middle of the seventh century.[110] This would be contemporary with the cemetery evidence for the first Saxons arriving in the area.

EXETER (*Isca Dumnoniorum*)   Probable

Description:
Civitas capital

Dating Evidence:
Several worn coins of Valens and Gratian (c.367-75)
One (chipped) coin of Magnus Maximus (c.387-88)
One coin of Theodosius, rev. VICTORIA AUGGG (c.388-92)
Several Byzantine copper coins of questionable provenance
Radiocarbon dating of two graves (420±70 and 490±80)
Sherds of late Roman *amphorae* (possibly Bv)

Sources:
Allan, J. et al. "Saxon Exeter." In *Anglo-Saxon Towns in Southern England*, ed. J. Haslam, pp. 385-414. Chichester: Phillimore, 1984.
Bidwell, Paul T. *Exeter Archaeological Reports: Vol. I, The Legionary Bath-House and Basilica and Forum at Exeter*. Exeter: Exeter Univ. Press, 1979.
—. *Roman Exeter: Fortress and Town*. Exeter: Exeter Museums Service, 1980.
Holbrook, Neil and Paul T. Bidwell. *Exeter Archaeological Reports: Vol. IV, Roman Finds from Exeter*. Exeter: Exeter Univ. Press, 1991.
Pearce, Susan. *The Kingdom of Dumnonia*. Padstow, Cornwall: Lodenek Press, 1978.

The forum basilica at Exeter underwent extensive remodelling in the latter part of the fourth century, and the new floor laid in the basilica contained a coin of Valens (c.367-75).[111] Though grass and weeds were apparently growing in the *palaestra* of the baths,[112] at least one Roman townhouse was built after the middle of the fourth century, with the insertion of a water trough overlaying a coin of c.363-67. Adjacent to this large house was a dump of oyster shells and a well-worn coin of Maximus (c.387-88), indicating probable activity at the site at the beginning of the fifth century.[113]

In the middle of the fifth century, the southern end of the forum and basilica was carefully demolished, and the stones were removed from the site in an orderly manner calling for some organization of manpower.[114] First a large quarry-pit, together with several smaller pits, were dug into the *curia* floor to extract clay for bronze-working.[115] Then the site was used as a cemetery, as excavators uncovered six inhumation graves which followed the alignment of the Roman buildings. Two of the graves yielded radiocarbon dates placing them in the fifth or sixth centuries, while the rest appeared to belong to the later Saxon minster church.[116]

Bidwell believes that these graves are part of a larger (yet to be fully excavated) Christian cemetery, indicating a fifth-century Christian community at Exeter which he describes as a "proto-monastery."[117] If these Christian graves were succeeded directly by the Saxon church and graveyard, it may signal continuity of occupation at Exeter.[118]

There is an intriguing reference to Exeter in the *Life of St. John the Almsgiver*, written in the early seventh century. A captain sailing from Alexandria with a cargo of corn is blown off course and lands in Britain, where he trades his cargo for Cornish tin (and some bronze *numisma*) and relieves a local famine. This reference has been taken to mean Exeter (or its port at Topsham), the first major Roman port reached by ships rounding the Iberian peninsula.[119] But it could also refer to some other Dumnonian port which had succeeded Exeter in the sub-Roman period. Castle Dore, near Fowey, may have become a new focal point for the post-Roman inhabitants of Dumnonia. The widespread occurance of Christian memorial stones with their Ogham script in West Devon and Cornwall suggests Welsh or Irish missionary activity in this area,[120] which was quickly solidifying into a westward-looking "Celtic" kingdom.

GLASTONBURY   Definite

Description:
Hilltop settlement; Christian site

Dating Evidence:
Imported pottery (Bi and Bii)
Byzantine censer (seventh century)

Sources:
Abrams, Leslie and James P. Carley, eds. *The Archaeology and History of Glastonbury Abbey*. Woodbridge, Suffolk: Boydell Press, 1991.
Ellis, P. "Excavations at Silver Street, Glastonbury, 1978." *PSANHS* 126 (1982): 17-31.
Radford, C.A. Ralegh. "Glastonbury Abbey." In *The Quest for Arthur's Britain*, ed. Geoffrey Ashe, pp. 97-110. New York: Paladin, 1971.
Radford, C.A. Ralegh and Michael J. Swanton. *Arthurian Sites in the West*. Exeter: Exeter Univ. Press, 1975.
Rahtz, Philip. "Excavations on Glastonbury Tor, Somerset, 1964-66." *Archaeological Journal* 127 (1970): 1-81.
—. "Glastonbury Tor." In *The Quest for Arthur's Britain*, ed. Geoffrey Ashe, pp. 111-22. New York: Paladin, 1971.
—. "Pagan and Christian by the Severn Sea." In *The Archaeology and History of Glastonbury Abbey*, ed. L. Abrams and J. Carley, pp. 3-38. Woodbridge, Suffolk: Boydell Press, 1991.
—. *English Heritage Book of Glastonbury*. London: Batsford, 1993.

Glastonbury has long been the focal point of Arthurian and early Christian tradition in Somerset. The two features that have received the most attention are Glastonbury Abbey, one of Britain's most magnificent pre-Reformation religious houses, and Glastonbury Tor, an enigmatic terraced hill which rises over 500 feet above the Somerset plains. The Tor has yielded the strongest evidence for sub-Roman occupation, but neither area has been fully excavated and little archaeological work has been done since the 1960s.

Ralegh Radford's excavations at Glastonbury Abbey were aimed at discovering the earliest religious activity on the site. An ancient cemetery of slab-lined graves was found near the remains of a timber structure thought to be the original church of St. Mary. Along with this small wattled building were found post-holes interpreted as the remains of wattled oratories, and the entire area was bounded on the east by a great bank and ditch thought to be a monastic *vallum*. Though no dating evidence was found at the Abbey, these features lay beneath later Saxon structures, leading Radford to interpret the site as a "Celtic" monastery based on Irish parallels.[121] More recent excavation on the precinct ditch uncovered wooden stakes which yielded radiocarbon determinations centering on the late sixth and seventh centuries.[122] Also found in this area was an eastern Mediterranean copper censer, of late sixth- or seventh-century date, which suggests that Glastonbury maintained Byzantine ecclesiastical contacts.[123]

Philip Rahtz's excavations on Glastonbury Tor have yielded much more evidence of sub-Roman occupation. Structures were found both on the summit of the Tor and on the terrace platforms, which were reached in medieval times by a series of steps cut into the bedrock approaching from the west.[124] Slight remains of wooden buildings were found associated with hundreds of animal bones (representing prepared joints of ham, beef, and mutton seemingly butchered elsewhere and brought to the site), charcoal, and burnt stones. A fenced-in eastern hollow yielded Roman tile,[125] a bone needle, an iron lamp-holder, and a mysterious stone cairn. The most important area was the south platform, where traces of a large timber building were found along with two hearths, crucibles and other evidence of metalworking, a dozen pieces of imported Mediterranean *amphorae*, and a carved bronze head (stylistically "Celtic").

Though the finds from the Tor are rich, their interpretation is rather difficult. Rahtz came up with four possibilities:

1) A pagan shrine.

2) A Christian hermitage.

3) The stronghold of a petty chieftain.

4) A defensive signal station, warning other British settlements of Saxon incursions.

Two north-south aligned graves (containing the leg bones of two individuals well under 20 years old) found on the Tor might support the first explanation, but there is no evidence of a late Roman temple at Glastonbury.[126] Though the early Christian associations with Glastonbury are many, Rahtz at first ruled out a Celtic monastery or hermitage because the quantity of meat bones seemed contrary to the ascetic lifestyle of "Celtic" monks. Because of the metalworking and Mediterranean imports, Rahtz favored the third interpretation, that the Tor was the fortress of a British chieftain, comparable to the craggy palaces of Dumbarton Rock and Dunadd.[127] However, others have persisted in preferring the monastic interpretation for the Tor occupation.[128] Evidence of meat-eating (i.e. animal bones) has since been found at such monastic sites as Iona and Whithorn, and now Rahtz himself is reconsidering the monastic model.[129] The Tor may then be the earliest attested eremitic monastic site in Britain, with the hermitage later brought under the control of the more accessible Abbey.[130] When the new rulers of Wessex began to patronize the Abbey in the seventh century, Glastonbury had long been venerated as a Christian holy site.[131]

HAM HILL   Possible

Description:
Hillfort (?)

Dating Evidence:
Late Roman pottery
Late Roman bronze rings
Several Roman coin hoards, fourth-century concentration
Coins of Valentinian II (375-92)
One coin of Arcadius
Possible imported *amphorae* (Bii)
Saxon shield boss, Evison type B (fifth/sixth century)

Sources:
Burrow, Ian. *Hillfort and Hill-Top Settlement in Somerset in the First to Eighth Centuries AD.* BAR British Series No. 91. Oxford: BAR Publishing, 1981.
Seaby, W.A. "The Iron Age Hillfort on Ham Hill." *Archaeological Journal* 107 (1950): 90-91.
—. "Coinage from Ham Hill in the County Museum, Taunton." *PSANHS* 95 (1950): 143-58.

Ham Hill is one of the largest contour hillforts in Britain, with an oblong plateau enclosed by a circuit of defenses five kilometers in length. However, imprecise and poorly recorded excavations from 1907 to 1930 have only given slight illumination to probable late Iron Age, Roman, and sub-Roman occupation. More recent casual finds have yielded an abundance of Roman material, including pottery and several coin hoards.[132] A 12-room Roman villa, associated with a coin series running from Carausius (287-293) to Valentinian II (375-392), has been partially excavated and seems to be part of an even larger complex of at least two phases.[133] No sub-Roman structures have been identified.

HIGH PEAK   Probable

Description:
Hillfort

Dating Evidence:
Imported pottery (Bi, Bii, and Biii)

Source:
Pollard, S.H.M. "Neolithic and Dark Age Settlements on High Peak, Sidmouth, Devon." *Proceedings of the Devonshire Archaeological Society* 23 (1966): 35-59.

The coastal hillfort at the top of High Peak in Devon has yielded evidence of Neolithic and sub-Roman occupations during excavations in 1871, 1929, and 1961-64. The only structures identified from the sub-Roman fort were a large single ditch, a rampart which formed the crest of the hill, and a small outer rampart on the eastern side of the site.[134] These may represent either a univallate or a bivallate contour hillfort, possibly overlooking a harbor. All three excavations turned up sherds of imported *amphorae* (dating to c.475-650 and representing several vessels), found at the crest of the hill, in the large ditch, and in the small rampart outside the ditch.[135] Along with the pottery were found animal bones (mostly ox and pig), a small bronze strap, a shale spindle whorl, and a whetstone. The large amounts of charcoal found in all the ditch fills and in the debris on the inner rampart suggest, to its most recent excavator, that the hillfort met a violent end at the hands of advancing Saxons.[136]

KILLIBURY Possible

Description:
Hillfort

Dating Evidence:
Imported pottery (2 fragments of Bi *amphorae*)

Source:
Miles, Henrietta. "Excavations at Killibury Hillfort, Egloshayle 1975-6." *Cornish Archaeology* 16 (1977): 89-121.

Killibury is a small, double-banked, concentric hillfort of the pre-Roman Iron Age. Limited excavation has revealed evidence that it was reoccupied in the sub-Roman period. Two small sherds, thought to belong to one Bi amphora (fifth or sixth century), were found in the base of the plough-soil.[137]

LUNDY ISLAND Probable

Description:
Cemetery; early Christian site

Dating Evidence:
Late Roman pottery (third and fourth centuries)
Unidentified imported bowl (400-800)
Four inscribed memorial stones (fifth to seventh century)

Sources:
Gardner, K. "Lundy." *Current Archaeology* 8 (1968): 196-202.
Thomas, A.C. "Lundy, 1969." *Current Archaeology* 16 (1969): 138-42.

Excavations at Beacon Hill on Lundy Island uncovered a cemetery and stone structures dating back to the Iron Age. Several stone-walled huts were associated with third and fourth century pottery, and one fragment belonged to a small red slipped wheel-made bowl, categorized by Thomas as a minor unidentified ware of the early post-Roman period.[138] The cemetery contained 30 cist-graves around an unidentified focus, with an enclosure probably dating to the late sixth century.[139] Four inscribed stones were found associated with the graves: two date to the fifth or early sixth century, one to the late fifth or sixth, and one to the seventh.[140] The seventh century memorial stone contained an inscribed cross, suggesting that by the seventh century the community using this cemetery was Christian.

MAIDEN CASTLE Probable

Description:
Hillfort; religious shrine

Dating Evidence:
One hoard of Constantinian coins (mid fourth century)
One hoard of coins with dates ranging to 367
Four gold *solidi* of Arcadius and Honorius

Sources:
Sharples, Niall M. *Maiden Castle*. London: Batsford/English Heritage, 1991.
—. *Maiden Castle: Excavations and Field Survey 1985-86*. London: English Heritage, 1991.
Wheeler, R.E.M. *Maiden Castle, Dorset*. Oxford: Oxford Univ. Press, 1943.

Maiden Castle, Britain's largest Celtic hillfort, was a political center for the Durotriges tribe before the Roman invasion. It was captured by Vespasian after a bloody massacre of its defenders, and consequently the Durotriges were encouraged to settle in nearby *Durnovaria* (Dorchester). In the late fourth century, sometime after 367, a Romano-Celtic temple was constructed on the hillfort's plateau.[141] Maiden Castle, with its large ramparts, may then have become an enclosed shrine similar to the temple at Lydney, possibly associated with a sub-Roman cemetery.[142] According to its first excavator, the temple at Maiden Castle had its floor replaced, suggesting "an existence prolonged well into the fifth century."[143] Thereafter, a nearby circular shrine may have replaced the Romano-Celtic temple.[144] The latest numismatic finds were from a hoard of four gold coins dating to about the first decade of the fifth century found near the temple.[145]

NETTLETON Probable

Description:
Late Roman temple

Dating Evidence:
500 coins dating from 333 to 402
Glass (late fourth and early fifth centuries)
A *plumbata* (early fifth century)
Metalworking debris
"Saxon" beads

Source:
Wedlake, W.J. *The Excavation of the Shrine of Apollo at*

Nettleton, Wiltshire 1956-71. London: Society of Antiquaries, 1982.

Excavations at the shrine of Apollo at Nettleton have revealed much and varied activity in the fourth and fifth centuries. Although the temple had become derelict in the second-half of the fourth century, sometime after 370 it was adapted for habitation and used as a farmstead until 392 or possibly later.[146] From knife or sword wounds found on skeltons at the site, the excavator believes that the homestead occupants were massacred as a result of a raid on the settlement sometime after 392.[147] Some 500 Roman coins, ranging in date from 333 to 402, were found along with other objects on the floor of the "West Lodge" (Building XVIII), and all had apparently been subjected to fire. One object associated with the coins was a *plumbata* or *martiobarbulus*, a lead-weighted feathered javelin head comparable to those found at Wroxeter (which date to the early fifth century).[148] Glass from this building has been assigned to the late fourth and early fifth centuries, and some of the beads found have been typed "Saxon." Reece, examining the coin evidence, sees occupation at the site continuing well into the fifth century.[149]

PHILLACK   Probable

Description:
Cemetery

Dating Evidence:
One sherd from a PRSW (Form 3) bowl (c.475-550)
One inscribed stone (c.600)

Sources:
Pearce, Susan. *The Kingdom of Dumnonia*. Padstow, Cornwall: Lodenek Press, 1978.
Thomas, Charles. "Christians, Chapels, Churches and Charters." *Landscape History* 11 (1989): 19-26.

Limited excavation at Phillack in west Cornwall has revealed a cemetery dated artifactually to the sub-Roman period.[150] The cemetery is enclosed and consists of inhumations in cist-graves oriented east-west, which suggests Christian use.[151] Dating evidence includes one sherd from a Phocean Red Slip Ware bowl and a nearby inscribed stone of c.600.[152] The evidence from Phillack compares to similar burial sites in the Scillies.[153]

THE SCILLY ISLES (*Sillina*)   Probable

Description:
Pagan shrine; early Christian site

Dating Evidence:
Imported pottery (Bii, Biv, and E ware)
Merovingian buckle and girdle hanger

Source:
Thomas, Charles. *Exploration of a Drowned Landscape: Archaeology and History of the Isles of Scilly*. London: Batsford, 1985.

These islets were once connected by the now submerged seabed to Cornwall. There is both literary and archaeological evidence that the Scillies were inhabited throughout the Roman period. The emperor Maximus exiled two Priscillianist heretics to Scilly in the fourth century. A Romano-Celtic pagan shrine found on Nor'nour yielded a late Roman treasure trove (including Roman coins of the late fourth century, glass, bronze finger-rings, pots, domestic pottery, bronze brooches, and clay goddess-figurines from Gaul), suggesting a lingering paganism to the beginning of the fifth century.[154] An early Christian wooden church was replaced by a stone chapel on St. Helen's, and the few graves excavated point to Christian cemeteries in the Scillies.[155] Scattered finds of imported pottery, found at Mary's Hill and Tean, and a Merovingian buckle and girdle hanger found at Tean, indicate commerical activity from the mid fifth to seventh centuries.[156]

SHEPTON MALLET   Possible

Description:
Small town; early Christian cemetery

Dating Evidence:
Bronze and silver coinage of the fourth century
Silver *Chi-Rho* amulet (c.400)
Late Roman pottery

Sources:
Leach, Peter. *Shepton Mallet: Romano-Britons and Early Christians in Somerset*. Birmingham: Birmingham Univ. Field Archaeology Unit, 1991.
Smith, R.F. *Roadside Settlements in Lowland Roman Britain*. BAR No. 157. Oxford: BAR Publishing, 1987.

Shepton Mallet was a (recently discovered) small Romano-British settlement, flourishing in the fourth century, situated on the Fosse Way between the larger towns of Bath and Ilchester. Excavations have revealed building-complexes, cobbled streets, and three small cemeteries. No town defenses, and no apparent planning scheme, meant that these cemeteries could be located close to inhabited buildings, and were perhaps privately-owned plots.[157] Most burials were in wooden coffins (only the iron nails survived) set into rock-cut graves, with few surviving grave goods.[158] The largest cemetery contained 17 inhumations aligned east-west within a ditched enclosure, and included one lead coffin and another burial accompanied by a silver cross-shaped amulet with a *Chi-Rho* symbol punched into it.[159] This positive identification of a Christian burial suggests a probable Christian community at Shepton Mallet in the later fourth century. Pottery and coinage take us up to about 400, but it is unclear how long after this the Christian community remained. There are some traces of timber structures cut into the latest levels of Roman buildings, suggesting post-Roman continuity, but dating these structures is not yet possible.[160]

SOUTH CADBURY (Cadbury Castle, "Camelot")   Definite

Description:
Hillfort

Dating Evidence:
Late Roman pottery
One coin of Honorius (c.393-402)
Imported pottery (PRSW, ARSW, Bi, Bii, Biv, Bmisc, and D ware)
Saxon gilt bronze button brooch (late fifth/early sixth century)
Saxon silver ring/brooch (late sixth century)

Sources:
Alcock, Leslie. "'By South Cadbury is that Camelot. . . .'" *Antiquity* 41 (1967): 50-53.
—. "A Reconnaissance Excavation at South Cadbury Castle, Somerset." *Antiquaries Journal* 47 (1967): 70-76.
—. "Cadbury Castle, 1967." *Antiquity* 43 (1968): 52-56.
—. "Excavations at South Cadbury Castle, 1967: a Summary Report." *Antiquaries Journal* 48 (1968): 6-17.
—. "South Cadbury Excavations, 1968." *Antiquity* 43 (1969): 52-56.
—. "Excavations at South Cadbury Castle, 1968: a Summary Report." *Antiquaries Journal* 49 (1969): 30-40.
—. "South Cadbury Excavations, 1969." *Antiquity* 44 (1970): 46-49.
—. "Excavations at South Cadbury Castle, 1969: a Summary Report." *Antiquaries Journal* 50 (1970): 14-25.
—. "Excavations at South Cadbury Castle, 1970: a Summary Report." *Antiquaries Journal* 51 (1971): 1-7.
—. *Arthur's Britain*. London: Penguin, 1971.
—. *'By South Cadbury is that Camelot.'* London: Thames and Hudson, 1972.
—. "Excavations at Cadbury-Camelot, 1966-70." *Antiquity* 46 (1972): 29-38.
—. "The Cadbury Castle Sequence in the First Millennium BC." *BBCS* 28 (1980): 656-718.
—. "Cadbury-Camelot: a Fifteen-Year Perspective." *Proceedings of the British Academy* 68 (1982): 355-88.
—. *Economy, Society and Warfare Among the Britons and Saxons*. Cardiff: Univ. of Wales Press, 1987.
Alcock, Leslie and Geoffrey Ashe. "Cadbury: is it Camelot?" In *The Quest for Arthur's Britain*, ed. Geoffrey Ashe, pp. 123-47. London: Paladin Press, 1968.
Burrow, Ian. *Hillfort and Hill-Top Settlement in Somerset in the First to Eighth Centuries AD*. BAR British Series No. 91. Oxford: BAR Publishing, 1981.
Radford, C.A. Ralegh and Michael J. Swanton. *Arthurian Sites in the West*. Exeter: Exeter Univ. Press, 1975.

The hill at South Cadbury, sometimes called "South Cadbury Castle" and "Cadbury-Camelot," was the site of one of the most publicized (and published) British excavations of the 1960s. The association with the fabled court of King Arthur was made by two prominent Tudor antiquarians, John Leland and William Camden, disregarding other sites traditionally associated with Arthur (e.g. Celliwic, Caerleon, Winchester) and the fact that "Camelot" was invented by Chrétien de Troyes or his successors in the twelfth and thirteenth centuries.[161] However, when ploughing on the hill in the 1950s turned up sherds of late Roman Mediterranean pottery, large-scale excavations soon commenced under the direction of Leslie Alcock, who had recently excavated the precedent-setting hillfort of Dinas Powys.

South Cadbury and Dinas Powys are both heavily fortified hilltop settlements which yielded strong evidence of sixth-century activity. There are other factors, however, which set South Cadbury apart from the Dinas Powys model. Most obvious is the sheer size of the hill: over 500 feet high, with steep sides defended by five massive ramparts, enclosing a plateau of about 18 acres. Burrow has estimated that it would have taken a force of about 870 men to defend and maintain the ramparts alone, compared to about 400-650 for the comparably sized Cadbury-Congresbury.[162] Also of significance is the extended sequence of activity at South Cadbury, noted by Alcock as one of the longest stratified sequences in western Europe.[163] Neolithic activity (beginning about 4500 BC) is indicated by pottery, flints, and both human and animal bones. A native farmstead occupied in the late Bronze Age (eighth century BC) fell to Iron Age invaders in the sixth or seventh century BC, when the first artificial ramparts were constructed. The Iron Age occupation was brought to a violent end shortly after the Roman invasion of AD 43, presumably during the campaigns of Vespasian, when the defenses were partly dismantled. Roman occupation (dated by coins, pottery, and military equipment) was slight until the third century, when a Romano-Celtic temple was constructed (out of timber) and frequently visited (coins range from 222-35 to 393-402). The defenses were repaired on a massive scale in the later fifth century and timber structures were constructed in the interior, all associated with Mediterranean imports. After a long period of abandonment, the fort was the site of a late Saxon *burg* and royal mint during the reign of Ethelred (beginning of the eleventh century), whence the gateways were rebuilt in stone. Finally, after Cnut's accession in 1017 the *burg* was abandoned and the hilltop given up to cultivation.

What Alcock terms the "Arthurian" period of occupation or Cadbury 11—the fifth and sixth centuries AD—is dated by the abundant finds of imported pottery, including fine red bowls, Mediterranean *amphorae*, and grey bowls and mortaria from the Bordeaux region. The quantity of sherds suggests a minimum vessel number comparable to that of Cadbury-Congresbury, and second only to Tintagel.[164] Sealed and scattered pottery were found in the post-holes and wall-trench of a rectangular structure on the summit of the hill. This building, about 19m long by 10m wide, was interpreted by Alcock as the principal building of the fort, probably a feasting hall.[165] Other post-holes suggest interior divisions and an antechamber. Such halls feature prominently in the poetry of the British Heroic Age, but only a few examples—notably Yeavering and Doon Hill—have been excavated and published.[166] Alcock, however, suggests that the model for the Cadbury hall was not the Germanic feasting hall but rather the aisled houses of villa complexes in later Roman Britain.[167] Though these were occasionally rebuilt in timber, a better model might be the massive timber building complexes constructed at the baths basilica in sub-Roman Wroxeter.[168] Only one other pottery-dated structure was excavated at Cadbury 11, that of a small (4m x 2m) rectangular building near the northern door of the hall which has been interpreted as a kitchen.[169] Finally, some of the smaller round houses previously attributed to the Iron Age may belong instead to Cadbury 11, with parallels at Cadbury-Congresbury and Buiston.[170]

Much of the imported pottery was found in association with the rebuilt defenses and the south-west gate. "The hill-top had been re-fortified with a timber fighting platform," writes Alcock, "faced with dressed stone and anchored down with rubble."[171] Stone for the ramparts had been quarried from derelict Roman buildings and was re-used unmortared in the non-Roman fashion of dry masonry. The absence of nails suggests wooden pegged joints were used, a somewhat sophisticated carpentry technique.[172] The timber gate-tower constructed at the south-west gate was seemingly based on the simple Roman auxiliary fort gate model, and showed signs of repair in the later sixth century.[173] It likely contained two double-leaved doors, an interior bridge, and possibly a light tower.[174] In all, the defensive circuit spans nearly twelve hundred meters, the same as the perimeter of the Iron Age fort. The size of the Cadbury defenses is without parallel among contemporary hillforts in Britain.

The size of South Cadbury's fortifications and the large quantity of imported pottery discovered there make it and Tintagel the two most significant sub-Roman occupation sites in the southwest. It should be noted that only six percent of the hillfort's summit was excavated by Alcock's team, and future excavation is likely to turn up a greater variety of structural and artifactual evidence.

TINTAGEL (*Durocornovium*?) Definite

Description:
Promontory hillfort; early Christian site

Dating Evidence:
Two inscribed milestones (third and fourth centuries)
Sherds of Oxford Red Color-Coated ware (fourth century)
10 bronze coins ranging from Tetricus I to Constantius II
Radiocarbon estimate from charcoal (calibrated: c.AD 403)
Archaeomagnetic date (AD 450-500)
Imported pottery (PRSW Form 3, ARSW, Bi, Bii, Biv, Bv, Bmisc, and D ware)
Glass fragments from drinking vessels
Slight traces of metalworking
Merovingian (?) ring-ornament

Sources:
Burrow, Ian C.G. "Tintagel—Some Problems." *Scottish Archaeological Forum* 5 (1973): 99-103.
Dark, Kenneth R. "The Plan and Interpretation of Tintagel." *CMCS* 9 (1985): 1-17.
—. Review of *Tintagel: Arthur and Archaeology*, by Charles Thomas. In *CMCS* 28 (1994): 103-4.
Morris, C.D. "Tintagel Castle Excavations 1990." Unpubl. interim statement, Univ. of Durham, 1990.
—. "Tintagel Island 1990, an Interim Report." *Cornish Archaeology* 30 (1991): 260-62.
Morris, C.D. *et al*. "Tintagel, Cornwall: The 1990 Excavations." *Antiquity* 64 (1990): 843-49.
Nowakowski, Jaqueline A. and Charles Thomas. *Excavations at Tintagel Parish Churchyard: Interim Report, Spring 1990*. Truro: Institute of Cornish Studies, 1990.
—. *Grave News from Tintagel. An Account of a Second Season of Archaeological Excavation at Tintagel Churchyard, Cornwall*. Truro: Institute of Cornish Studies, 1992.
Padel, O.J. "Tintagel—An Alternative View." In *A Provisional List of Imported Pottery in Post-Roman Western Britain and Ireland*, C. Thomas, pp. 28-29. Truro: Institute of Cornish Studies, 1981.
Radford, C.A. Ralegh. *Tintagel Castle*. London: HMSO, 1939; English Heritage, 1985.
—. "Imported Pottery Found at Tintagel, Cornwall." In *Dark Age Britain*, ed. D.B. Harden, pp. 59-67. London: Methuen, 1956.
—. "Romance and Reality in Cornwall: Tintagel." In *The Quest for Arthur's Britain*, ed. Geoffrey Ashe, pp. 59-70. New York: Paladin, 1971.
Radford, C.A. Ralegh and Michael J. Swanton. *Arthurian Sites in the West*. Exeter: Exeter Univ. Press, 1975.
Thomas, Charles. "East and West: Tintagel, Early Mediterranean Imports and the Insular Church." In *The Early Church in Western Britain and Ireland*, ed. S. Pearce, pp. 17-34. BAR British Series No. 102. Oxford: BAR Publishing, 1982.
—. "Tintagel Castle." *Antiquity* 62 (1988): 421-34.
—. "The Context of Tintagel. A New Model for the Diffusion of Post-Roman Mediterranean Imports." *Cornish Archaeology* 27 (1990): 7-25.
—. *Tintagel: Arthur and Archaeology*. London: English Heritage/Batsford, 1993.
Thomas, Charles, ed. *Tintagel Papers*. Cornish Studies Vol. 16. Redruth: Institute of Cornish Studies, 1988.

The picturesque ruins of the Norman castle at Tintagel have inspired writers from Geoffrey of Monmouth to Tennyson who have helped add "King Arthur's Castle" to the tourist's map. More recently, archaeologists and historians have begun to unravel the complex history of the site, whose "Dark Age" phase is showing signs of activity on a grander scale than the legends themselves.

Beyond the inner ward of the Norman castle, on the high protruding headland called "Tintagel Island," lay the remains of several small rectangular structures made of stone and slate. Radford's excavation of these structures in the 1930s revealed thousands of sherds of imported pottery, then known as "Tintagel ware." Because this pottery dated to the fifth to seventh centuries and was used primarily for the transportation of wine and oil, Radford interpreted the headland settlement as a remote Celtic monastery.

The monastic model for Tintagel was commonly accepted until the 1970s, when Ian Burrow and others began casting doubts on Radford's interpretation of the stone huts, whose number has now grown from 30 to over 100.[175] Because Tintagel does not appear as a monastery in Cornish hagiography, and because no early Christian church or cemetery have been found at the castle site, archaeologists now doubt that the stone huts are monastic "cells." Some are likely barracks belonging to the Norman castle, while others—on both the plateau of the headland and on its terraces—are multi-period, including drystone buildings contemporary with the imported pottery.[176]

The monastic model is now being replaced by a secular interpretation of the Tintagel settlement. The new models proposed are 1) a fortress or royal seat, and 2) an international port of trade. The first model is supported more by linguistic and literary evidence than archaeology. The name "Tintagel" is thought to derive from the Cornish *tin/din*, "fort," and *tagell*, "neck or constriction."[177] Thomas believes that Tintagel's original identity as a castle or fortress was perpetuated by the Romans, making it the coastal *Durocornovium* ("fort of the Cornovii") listed in the *Ravenna Cosmography*.[178] Two inscribed Roman milestones have been found in Tintagel, as well as Roman coins and both commercial and locally made pottery of the third and fourth centuries.[179] Whatever role it played during the Roman occupation, later tradition made Tintagel the fortified seat of the rulers of Dumnonia, including Mark and Tristan. This tradition, in turn, may have had something to do with the location here of the twelfth- or thirteenth-century Norman castle which Geoffrey of Monmouth linked with Arthur.[180]

The second model holds that Tintagel was a major late and sub-Roman port of trade, perhaps occupied only seasonally. This theory is based primarily on the enormous amount of imported pottery which has been (and still is being) uncovered on the headland. More fine pottery and amphoras—over 300 vessels in all—have been found at Tintagel than at any other site in Britain and Ireland.[181] Slight traces of metalworking found at Tintagel support the widely-held view that Cornish tin was traded for the imports,[182] which Dark suggests passed first through Frankish middle-men (hence the possibly Merovingian ring-ornament) before arriving in Britain.[183] Minor excavation on the headland in the 1980s began to uncover evidence of associated structures, including a possible sub-Roman wharf below the Iron Gate and a court beneath the Norman hall of the Inner Ward.[184] In the Lower Ward, on the mainland, excavation revealed two hearths, a well-built oven, a multitude of butchered and cooked bones, and imported glass, pottery, and metalwork, suggesting intensive food preparation and cooking at the site.[185] One of the clay hearths yielded an archaeomagnetic date of AD 450-500 (at a 68% confidence level).[186]

Charles Thomas has recently re-evaluated the evidence at Tintagel for English Heritage.[187] He argues that there are too many geographic problems at Tintagel headland—a restricted location, vulnerability to gales and salt-laden spray, meagre and shallow soil cover, a limited water supply—to have made it suitable for year-round habitation, so that during the period of its imports (about 450 to 650) it is more likely to have been inhabited only periodically, perhaps solely during the summer months.[188] However, the construction of a ditch-and-rampart line across its only point of landward access, along with the metal-working and ostentatious signs of wealth, make it an ideal candidate for a fortress. Thomas sees Tintagel Island as a stronghold of the post-Roman kings of Dumnonia, but one used only periodically as part of an irregular sequence of dynastic visitations, where food as well as goods required for overseas trade were brought to the king under a system of enforced obligations.[189] Such itinerant kings are well-attested in the early medieval world, the theory being that it was easier to take the larger royal households to the food than it was to maintain them in one permanent location.[190]

Even if the settlement on the headland turns out to be thoroughly secular, there is still strong evidence for early Christianity at Tintagel. Thomas led two seasons of excavation at the Tintagel Parish Churchyard, which is on the mainland not far from the castle. His team uncovered two slate-lined graves, two rock-covered burial mounds, and one memorial pillar; associated imported pottery and a cross on one of the slates identify the site as early Christian (400-600).[191] Near the graves were found traces of open-air fires, the remains of which yielded a (calibrated) radiocarbon date centering on AD 403.[192] Thomas suggests that the fire and pottery are the remains of a funeral meal held at the Christian cemetery, a custom common at this time on the continent.[193] Remains of a low bank of earth and stones surrounding the yard yielded a sherd of ARSW, suggesting that an enclosure was added to the cemetery in the later sixth century.[194] Its excavators see Tintagel Churchyard as an important burial ground "contemporary and associated with the post-Roman use of the Island."[195]

TRETHURGY   Probable

Description:
Circular fortification (a "round")

Dating Evidence:
Grass-marked pottery
Imported pottery (PRSW, Bi, Bii, Biv, Bmisc, and E ware)
Imported glass

Source:
Miles, H. and T. "Excavations at Trethurgy, St. Austell, Interim Report." *Cornish Archaeology* 12 (1973): 25-29.

Trethurgy is a univallate hill-slope enclosure, one of many circular walled and ditched fortifications common in south-western Britain refered to as Cornish "rounds." Trethurgy has produced locally-made pottery and some 50 sherds from imported *amphorae*, representing four different styles of vessels, along with sherds of Phocean Red Slip Ware and E ware from Gaul.[196] The pottery range suggests a period of occupation throughout the fifth and sixth centuries.[197] Also found was a tin ingot, which lends support to the theory that Cornish tin was exchanged for the Mediterranean and Gaulish imports.[198]

WELLS   Possible

Description:
Mausoleum

Sources:
Morris, Richard. *The Church in British Archaeology*. CBA Research Report No. 47. London: CBA, 1983.
Rodwell, W.J. *Wells Cathedral: Excavations and Discoveries*. Wells: Friends of Wells Cathedral, 1979; rev. ed. 1980.

Recent excavation at Wells Cathedral has revealed a late or sub-Roman stone building standing beside the first Anglo-Saxon church. The building has been tentatively identified as a mausoleum.[199]

WEST HILL ULEY   Probable

Description:
Romano-Celtic temple

Dating Evidence:
32 bronze coins of Arcadius
8 silver and bronze coins of Honorius
6 "House of Theodosius" bronze coins
Glass drinking cups (fourth century)
Grass-tempered ware
Shell-tempered ware
Oxfordshire ware
Window glass (seventh to ninth century)

Sources:
Ellison, Ann. *Excavations at West Hill Uley: 1977. The Romano-British Temple—Interim Report*. Bristol: Committee for Rescue Archaeology in Avon, Gloucestershire and Somerset, 1978.
—. *Excavations at West Hill Uley: 1977-79. A Native, Roman and Christian Ritual Complex of the First Millennium AD—Second Interim Report*. Bristol: Committee for Rescue Archaeology in Avon, Gloucestershire and Somerset, 1980.
—. "Natives, Romans and Christians on West Hill, Uley: An Interim Report on the Excavation of a Ritual Complex of the First Millenium AD." In *Temples, Churches and Religion in Roman Britain*, ed. W. Rodwell, pp. 305-28. BAR British Series No. 77. Oxford: BAR Publishing, 1980.
Woodward, Ann and Peter Leach. *The Uley Shrines: Excavation of a Ritual Complex on West Hill, Uley, Gloucestershire 1977-79*. London: English Heritage/British Museum, 1993.

A major rescue excavation in 1977 uncovered a temple complex on West Hill in Uley. Coinage indicates a series of religious structures built on the site beginning in the LPRIA and continuing in the Roman and post-Roman periods. The major feature was a small Romano-Celtic temple consisting of stone-walled concentric rectangles with associated bronze coinage and other votive objects. Coin evidence suggests that the temple was built in the second quarter of the fourth century and demolished c.400. This occurred with a systematic dismantling of the buildings and the careful removal of the stonework.[200]

Excavation further disclosed at least three phases of post-temple structures, associated with Theodosian coinage and various types of Romano-British pottery. The first of these structures, represented by large post pits and beam slots cut through the demolished remains of the stone temple, has been interpreted as a double-aisled timber basilica (11m x 9.2m), probably a church, constructed sometime after the last coins were deposited (c.402).[201] No apse was identified, but an attached polygonal structure may have served as a baptistry (with a conjectured altar).[202] In the late fifth or sixth century, a perimeter bank was built around the complex, with two foundations of dry stone footings and postholes at the north end possibly representing gate towers with stair-turrets.[203]

In the late sixth or early seventh century, the timber basilica was dismantled and a smaller stone structure was erected over the northeastern corner of the basilica.[204] This rectangular masonry building was later given an apse, and has been interpreted as a two-cell chapel. Associated with the chapel were ten fragments of blue-green window glass, some containing dark red streaks, which have parallels with Anglo-Saxon churches and are thus most likely post-Roman.[205] Also possibly connected with the stone church is a polygonal open-sided structure south of the church with mortared stone footings, interpreted as an open "screen" roofed with re-used Roman tiles.[206] The incorporation of the pagan altar and a statue of Mercury into the sub-Roman structures' walls lends support to the excavators' explanation of Uley as a Christian takeover of a pagan shrine.[207]

WINCHESTER (*Venta Belgarum*)   Probable

Description:
Civitas capital

Dating Evidence:
One coin of Valentinian I (364-75)
One bronze coin, "House of Theodosius" issue (c.388-402)
Sherds of Romano-British pottery (late fourth century)

Sources:
Biddle, M. "Excavations at Winchester, 1971: Tenth and Final Report, Part I." *Antiquaries Journal* 55 (1975): 96-126.
—. "Excavations at Winchester, 1971: Tenth and Final Report, Part II." *Antiquaries Journal* 55 (1975): 295-337.
—. "The Study of Winchester: Archaeology and History in a British Town." *Proceedings of the British Academy* 69 (1983): 93-135.
Clarke, Giles. *The Roman Cemetery at Lankhills*. Winchester Studies No. 3: Pre-Roman and Roman Winchester, Part 2. Oxford: Clarendon Press, 1979.

A late Roman cemetery at Lankhills, just outside of Winchester's north gate, has yielded an abundance of graves dating to the late fourth or early fifth century.[208] Some of these graves were cut into by sub-Roman structures, labeled by the excavators Features 24, 25, and 26. Features 25 and 26 appear to have been bedding-trenches for plants forming the boundary of a garden.[209] While there was some decay in street and drain maintenance, there were also metallings (of inferior quality) and new timber structures which encroached on the carriageways.[210] Wacher believes the citizenry began building their houses on top of the paved city streets because they provided a firm, well-drained foundation.[211] "These metallings and structures," comments Esmonde Cleary, "however much they represent a decline in standards, also represent a continuation of population."[212]

Wales

ABERFFRAW   Possible

Description:
Auxiliary fort (?); princely stronghold

Dating Evidence:
Roman pottery

Sources:
Edwards, N. "Aberffraw." In *Early Medieval Settlements in Wales 400-1100*, ed. N. Edwards and A. Lane, pp. 18-21. Cardiff: Univ. of Wales Press, 1988.
White, Richard B. "Excavations at Aberffraw, Anglesey, 1973 and 1974." *BBCS* 28 (1979): 319-42.

Excavation at Aberffraw, on Anglesey, revealed what appeared to be—because of associated pottery—a late Roman auxiliary fort. Its stone rampart was rebuilt, according to the excavator, possibly as a *ballista* platform, "in the fifth or sixth centuries by the founders of what was to be one of Gwynedd's most successful dynasties."[213] Edwards does not believe that Aberffraw was a Roman fort, but rather that its construction was wholly the work of the kings of Gwynedd in the fifth century.[214] An inscribed lead coffin, bearing the *Alpha* and *Omega* (and possibly the *Chi-Rho*) symbols, suggests a wealthy Christian community in early post-Roman Anglesey.[215]

BREIDDIN/NEW PIECES   Possible

Description:
Hillfort

Dating Evidence:
Late or post-Roman glass bead
Fragment from a glass beaker (fifth/sixth century)

Source:
Musson, C.R. *et al. The Breiddin Hillfort. A Later Prehistoric Settlement in the Welsh Marches.* CBA Report No. 76. London: CBA, 1991.

The Breiddin is one of the largest hillforts in Britain, its inner rampart enclosing 28 ha. A probably late or post-Roman glass bead was found on the enclosure. The globular bead is of crackled turquoise glass.[216] Excavations in the 1930s at nearby New Pieces, a small bivallate enclosure, yielded one—perhaps two—pieces of glass dated to the fifth or sixth century. The more distinctive piece is from a colorless or pale green glass vessel, probably a tall beaker.[217]

CAERLEON (*Isca*)   Probable

Description:
Legionary fortress

Dating Evidence:
Imported pottery (Bv)
Radiocarbon date of burial (c.660-940)

Sources:
Boon, George C. *Isca: the Roman Legionary Fortress at Caerleon.* Cardiff: National Museum of Wales, 1972.
Evans, D.R. and V.M. Metcalf. *Roman Gates, Caerleon.* Oxbow Monograph No. 15. Oxford: Oxbow, 1992.
Evans, E.M. "Caerleon, Mill Street Suburb." *Archaeology of Wales* 26 (1986): 46-47.
Lane, Alan. "Caerleon." In *Early Medieval Settlements in Wales AD 400-1100*, ed. N. Edwards and A. Lane, p. 34. Cardiff: Univ. of Wales Press, 1988.
Metcalf, V.M. "Caerleon, 'Roman Gates.'" *Archaeology of Wales* 21 (1981): 52-53.
Zienkiewicz, J.D. *The Legionary Fortress Baths at Caerleon.* Cardiff: Amgueddfa Genedlaethol Cymru, 1986.

The fortress of *Isca* was systematically dismantled after its legion was removed c.260. Thereafter civilian occupation continued in Caerleon until at least 375, and an early Christian tradition in the city is suggested by the literary sources.[218] Some time after 354, two round-ended buildings (K and L) were constructed over the *via vicinaria* and the verandah of barrack block A.[219] Building K, which has left the most traces, was originally 7.2m x 4.5m with "two post holes flanking a *tegula* which had been reused as part of a threshold," stones walls (one of which concealed a late military bronze belt fitting) and partitions, and a floor of well-laid rubble paving.[220] Inserted under the paved floor was a single female inhumation burial, the skeletal remains yielding a radiocrabon date of c.660-940.[221] "The need for extra buildings in a vernacular style may imply," according to the excavators, "a considerable population for Caerleon during the earlier part of the [medieval] period."[222] Giraldus Cambrensis, writing in the twelfth century, described baths, temples, water conduits, hypocausts, and an amphitheatre which were still standing at Caerleon in his day.[223]

CAERNARVON (*Segontium*)   Probable

Description:
Roman fort

Dating Evidence:
One clipped *siliqua*, probably of Theodosius (379-95)

Four penannular brooches (fifth century)
Metalworking debris

Sources:
Casey, P.J. "Excavations Outside the North-East Gate of Segontium." *Archaeologia Cambrensis* 123 (1974): 54-77.
Casey, P.J. and J.L. Davies. *Segontium. Excavations at Caernarfon 1976, an Interim Report*. Durham: Univ. of Durham, 1977.
—. *Excavations at Segontium (Caernarfon) Roman Fort, 1975-79*. London: CBA, 1993.
Davies, J.L. "Segontium, Caernarfon." In *Early Medieval Settlements in Wales AD 400-1100*, ed. N. Edwards and A. Lane, pp. 115-16. Cardiff: Univ. of Wales Press, 1988.
Laing, Lloyd. "Segontium and the Roman Occupation of Wales." In *Studies in Celtic Survival*, ed. L. Laing, pp. 57-60. BAR No. 37. Oxford: BAR Publishing, 1977.
Jones, M.L. *Society and Settlement in Wales and the Marches, 500 BC to AD 1100*. 2 vols. BAR No. 121. Oxford: BAR Publishing, 1984.

The Roman fort of Segontium, which underwent extensive internal modifications in the fourth century, appears to have been manned up to about 410 (or that time when payment failed to reach the frontier).[224] Sub-Roman activity is indicated by a new sentry-box built in the SE guardroom of the SW gateway, and two penannular brooches dating stylistically to the fifth century.[225] An early medieval church was founded just outside of Segontium, at Llanbeblig, and ordered government in this area is indicated by terms like *civis* and *magistratus* inscribed on the sixth-century Penmachno stone.[226]

CAERWENT (*Venta Silurum*)   Probable

Description:
Civitas capital

Dating Evidence:
Seven Theodosian coin hoards (coin range 388-402)
Seven late Roman buckles
Two lead-weighted javelin heads (*martiobarbuli*)
One fine zoomorphic penannular brooch
Radiocarbon dating of graves (fifth to eighth centuries)
Class G penannular brooch
Two spiral pins (seventh century)

Sources:
Davies, Wendy. "Roman Settlements and Post-Roman Estates in South-East Wales." In *The End of Roman Britain*, ed. P.J. Casey, pp. 153-73. BAR No. 71. Oxford: BAR Publishing, 1979.
Farley, M. "A 600 Metre Long Section Through Caerwent." *BBCS* 31 (1984): 209-50.
Knight, J.K. and Alan Lane. "Caerwent." In *Early Medieval Settlements in Wales 400-1100*, ed. N. Edwards and A. Lanes, pp. 35-38. Cardiff: Univ. of Wales Press, 1988.
Reece, R. "Numerical Aspects of Roman Coin Hoards in Britain." In *Coins and the Archaeologist*, ed. P.J. Casey and R. Reece, pp. 78-94. BAR No. 4. Oxford: BAR Publishing, 1974.

Caerwent began as a fort and developed into a large town and *civitas* center. In the middle of the fourth century, the town defenses were strengthened with the addition of at least eleven external towers, heptagonal in shape and irregularly spaced.[227] Also at this time both the south and north gates at Caerwent were blocked, seemingly in answer to some external threat.[228] Several Theodosian coin hoards were found at Caerwent, deposited after buildings had collapsed and possibly—as has been suggested by Reece—as late as the second or third quarter of the fifth century.[229]

Graffiti scratched on the walls of the curia in the basilica have been assigned to the fifth century, and the forum remained in use some time after that.[230] Drains were built running through the blocked-up gates, suggesting that the baths were still operating for some time until they collapsed and were replaced by another structure, possibly a church.[231] Though this interpretation has been questioned, four other stone buildings have been identified recently as early medieval and may have belonged to the sixth-century monastery founded by the Irish Saint Tathan.[232] Stylistic analysis of jewelry found in the town confirms occupation and activity during this period.[233]

The excavation of a cemetery just outside the walls of Caerwent revealed further evidence of sub-Roman occupation. Radiocarbon dates taken from the graves show that the people of Caerwent continued to be buried in this cemetery in the fifth and sixth centuries; in fact, the continuity extends to the eighth or ninth century when the settlement was clearly monastic.[234] One interesting burial contained a Roman coin (c.335-48) and a late Roman bracelet, yet radiocarbon analysis indicated a date of c.540-770. "If this is correct," comment Knight and Lane, "it implies the continuing use of Roman objects well into the early medieval period."[235]

CALDEY ISLAND   Possible

Description:
Early Christian site (?)

Dating Evidence:
Imported pottery (PRSW and E ware)
Early Christian inscribed stone (fifth or sixth century)

Sources:
Campbell, Ewan. "New Finds of Post-Roman Imported Pottery and Glass from South Wales." *Archaeologia Cambrensis* 138 (1989): 59-66.
Evans, G.E. "Caldey Island: Discovery of Stone-Lined Graves." *Transactions of the Carmarthenshire Antiquarian Society* 12 (1918): 43.
Leach, A.L. "Ancient Graves on the Isle of Caldey." *Archaeologia Cambrensis* (1918): 174-75.

Two long-cist burials were found in early excavations on Caldey Island, near St. David's Church and the medieval priory respectively.²³⁶ An early Christian ogham inscribed stone (*ECMW* No. 301) found near the priory could support the later hagiographic evidence of a sixth-century monastery founded on the site of the later priory by Abbot Pyro.²³⁷

More recently, Ewan Campbell has identified two sherds of imported pottery found in the vicinity of St. David's Church.²³⁸ One is a sherd of Phocaean Red Slip Ware imported from Asia Minor in the mid fifth or sixth century; the other is a sherd of E ware, probably from a Merovingian jar imported in the seventh century. Campbell believes that these imports belonged to a secular settlement at St. David's associated with the nearby landing place and perhaps the cist burials, and contemporary with the sixth-century monastic (?) foundation at the priory.²³⁹

CAPEL MAELOG   Possible

Description:
Hillfort

Dating Evidence:
Calibrated radiocarbon dates (AD 260-597 and AD 660-980)

Sources:
Britnell, W.J. "Capel Maelog, Llandrindod Wells, Powys: Excavations 1984-87." *Medieval Archaeology* 34 (1990): 27-96.
James, Heather. "Early Medieval Cemeteries in Wales." In *The Early Church in Wales and the West*, ed. N. Edwards and A. Lane, pp. 90-103. Oxbow Monograph No. 16. Oxford: Oxbow, 1992.

Capel Maelog is a small univallate enclosure. Ditch fills under a possibly sub-Roman rectangular enclosure yielded two calibrated radiocarbon dates, centering on the fifth and ninth centuries respectively.²⁴⁰

COYGAN CAMP   Probable

Description:
Promontory fort

Dating Evidence:
Roman pottery (late second to late fourth centuries)
Imported pottery (PRSW and Bi)
Two crucibles
Three spear-heads
One dagger

Sources:
Campbell, Ewan. "Coygan Camp." In *Early Medieval Settlements in Wales AD 400-1100*, ed. N. Edwards and A. Lane, pp. 44-46. Cardiff: Univ. of Wales Press, 1988.
Wainwright, G.J. *Coygan Camp*. Cardiff: Cambrian Archaeological Association, 1967.

Coygan Camp is an Iron Age promontory fort which has shown signs of occupation in the Roman and early medieval periods. The fort was defended on its north and west sides by a stone-built rampart with revetments on both sides. Four structures ("huts") have been identified, of both stone and timber construction, but no finds were associated with them to allow for dating.²⁴¹

There is an abundance of finds, however, from other areas of the site. Coins and pottery show that the Roman period occupation extends from at least the second to the fourth century.²⁴² Sixth-century occupation is attested by the presence of imported pottery—one sherd of a Bi amphora and five sherds of Phocaean Red Slip Ware—which came from complete vessels and pre-date the rampart tumble.²⁴³ Other finds of possible early medieval date include two crucibles, a bronze ingot, a dagger, and three spear-heads of non-Roman type. Campbell believes that the range of finds suggests continuity of occupation from the Roman to early medieval periods, while "the imported pottery indicates that there must have been a high-status site at Coygan in the sixth century."²⁴⁴

DEGANNWY CASTLE (*Arx Decantorum*)   Definite

Description:
Hillfort

Dating Evidence:
Coins ranging from Gallienus (260-68) to Valens (364-78)
Late Roman pottery (fourth century)
Imported pottery (Bi and Bmisc)
Post-Roman glass (?)

Sources:
Alcock, Leslie. "Excavations at Degannwy Castle, Caernarvonshire, 1961-6." *Archaeological Journal* 124 (1967): 190-201.
Lane, Alan. "Degannwy Castle." In *Early Medieval Settlements in Wales AD 400-1100*, ed. N. Edwards and A. Lane, pp. 50-53 and Appendix 1. Cardiff: Univ. of Wales Press, 1988.

The medieval fortifications of Degannwy Castle straddle two craggy hilltops overlooking Conwy Bay. Leslie Alcock's excavations between 1961 and 1966 revealed traces of early medieval structures beneath the thirteenth century castle, especially on the western hill. A drystone wall and two trenches were uncovered on the eastern side of the hill, though this may have enclosed the entire summit. The drystone wall is not closely datable, though datable glass and pottery were found (unstratified) very near it.²⁴⁵

Artifactual evidence suggests occupation in the Roman period and a long sequence throughout the medieval period. Late Roman finds include a coin sequence extending from Gallienus (260-68) to Valens (364-78) and pottery—"calcite-gritted material and a 'Dinorben' bowl"—of similar date.²⁴⁶ Early medieval objects include one sherd from a Bi amphora, datable to the late fifth to mid sixth century, and about a dozen fragments from "B miscellaneous" amphoras.²⁴⁷ These were found associated with a fragment of possibly post-Roman glass.

Though there is an absence of coins of the period 330-48, Roman occupation at Degannwy is likely to extend from the

260s to the 370s.[248] The imported pottery argues for early sixth-century occupation, while there is an absence of material to argue for continuity. Later tradition associates Degannwy Castle with Maelgwn of Gwynedd, one of the *tyranni* denounced by Gildas. Though the tradition is a strong one, it may be rather late.[249] Likewise, an entry in the *Annales Cambriae* for the year 812 states that "The citadel of the Canti (*Decantorum arx*) is struck by lightning and burnt," and this is usually identified with Degannwy.[250]

DINAS EMRYS   Definite

Description:
Hillfort

Dating Evidence:
Gilt-bronze studs (late or post-Roman)
Late Roman pottery (fourth century)
Seven glass vessels (c.400)
Imported potttery (Biv and E ware)
Chi-Rho stamped plate (sixth century)

Sources:
Breese, C.E. "The Fort at Dinas Emrys." *Archaeologia Cambrensis* 85 (1930): 342-54.
Campbell, Ewan. "Dinas Emrys." In *Early Medieval Settlements in Wales AD 400-1100*, ed. N. Edwards and A. Lane, pp. 54-57 and Appendix 1. Cardiff: Univ. of Wales Press, 1988.
Laing, Lloyd and Jennifer. "Scottish and Irish Metalwork and the *conspiratio barbarica*." *PSAS* 116 (1986): 211-21.
Savory, H.N. "Excavations at Dinas Emrys, Beddgelert, Caernarvonshire, 1954-6." *Archaeologia Cambrensis* 109 (1960): 13-77.

The craggy hillfort of Dinas Emrys lies on one of the principal routes through Snowdonia. Excavations in 1910 and in the 1950s revealed several stone walls and revetted platforms surrounding a small summit. On the summit were found the stone foundations of an oval structure, a square pool or cistern, several postholes (possibly belonging to a palisade), and other structures of indeterminate date and function.

The artifactual evidence ranges from the early Roman to the medieval period. Roman period finds include pottery, glass, an iron brooch, and three "Donside" terrets (rein-rings from a chariot). Late Roman and early medieval finds include gilt-bronze studs, mortaria (late third or fourth century), color-coated wares and calcite-gritted vessels (late fourth century), at least seven glass vessels, a two-handled Biv amphora (fifth or sixth century), and a roundel cut from a pottery sherd with a *Chi-Rho* pattern on it (sixth century).

Dating the periods of occupation at Dinas Emrys has proven to be difficult and controversial. The early material, thought to belong to Iron Age or early Roman occupation, may have been brought to the site at a later date.[251] Late Roman occupation seems certain—because of the abundance of pottery and glass—and probably spans the fourth century. Early medieval occupation is indicated by the imported pottery (fifth to sixth centuries), and both the middle and main ramparts rest on late Roman material.[252]

More questions surround the nature of the pool, discovered in Savory's excavations. The 1910 excavation sought the legendary sinking tower of Vortigern, but uncovered the remains of a Norman castle instead. When Savory uncovered the pool and found it contained fifth- or sixth-century imported pottery, it was hard not to see it as the pool where Vortigern is confronted by the prophetic boy in the *Historia Brittonum*. Radiocarbon dating and a sherd of medieval pottery seem to contradict this, though this material may be intrusive.[253] Even more perplexing is the presence of some 33 posts erected within the pool, which must have seen a long and complex sequence of activity.

DINAS POWYS   Definite

Description:
Hillfort

Dating Evidence:
Imported pottery (PRSW, Bi, Bii, D and E ware)
"Anglo-Saxon" and continental glass (bowls and beakers)
Bonework, trinkets, and metalworking debris
Mold for a zoomorphic penannular brooch (sixth century)

Sources:
Alcock, Leslie. *Dinas Powys, an Iron Age, Dark Age and Early Medieval Settlement in Glamorgan*. Cardiff: Univ. of Wales Press, 1963.
—. "Refortified or Newly Fortified? The Chronology of Dinas Powys." *Antiquity* 54 (1980): 231-32.
—. *Economy, Society and Warfare Among the Britons and Saxons*. Cardiff: Univ. of Wales Press, 1987.
Campbell, Ewan. "Dinas Powys." In *Early Medieval Settlements in Wales AD 400-1100*, ed. N. Edwards and A. Lane, pp. 58-61. Cardiff: Univ. of Wales Press, 1988.
—. "A Blue Glass Squat Jar from Dinas Powys, South Wales." *BBCS* 36 (1989): 239-45.
Gilchrist, R. "A Re-appraisal of Dinas Powys." *Medieval Archaeology* 32 (1988): 50-62.
Pierce, G.O. *The Place-Names of Dinas Powys Hundred*. Cardiff: Univ. of Wales Press, 1968.

Dinas Powys, near Cardiff in Glamorganshire, is a small hilltop settlement surrounded by crude defensive earthworks. Leslie Alcock's excavations in the 1950s, extensively documented, made Dinas Powys the classic site of post-Roman Celtic archaeology. In the thirty years since the excavations were first published, Alcock and others have reassessed and reinterpreted the nature of the sub-Roman settlement at Dinas Powys in light of new discoveries at similarly occupied hillforts.

The post-Roman occupation of Dinas Powys does not represent the re-use or refortification of an Iron Age hillfort. Though some Iron Age pottery was discovered at the site, no Iron Age structures were recognized.[254] Excavation did reveal an abundance of Roman-period material, including colored glass and window-glass (first to second century), Samian ware (second century), a Roman brick, a La Tène brooch (first century), and tools for the manufacture of shale armlets.[255] Because these objects were not associated with Roman-period structures, Alcock believes that they were brought to the site as "mementos" in the fifth and sixth centuries. Others have questioned Alcock's "mementos theory." Rahtz has suggested that the Roman fine table- and glass-wares were hoarded heirlooms that came into use again when pottery and glass became extremely scarce in late fifth-century Britain.[256] The Laings believe that the Romano-British material, because it falls mostly into the first and second centuries, must represent contemporary occupation of some sort.[257] They would even date one of the earthen banks to the early Roman period, which could throw off the chronology of the sub-Roman phases.

Alcock's sub-Roman phase—which he labels "Phase 4/Early Christian"—has three further divisions (A, B, and C) and spans the fifth through seventh centuries. Phase 4A (fifth century) is represented by three industrial hearths (with associated metal-working debris), fence holes, one defensive bank and ditch, an incomplete timber structure, a child's grave, and the earliest imported pottery (PRSW). Phase 4B (fifth to seventh centuries) showed continued industrial activity, the construction of two stone houses (inferred from two rectangular gullies), and the latest pottery imports (E ware). Phase 4C (seventh to eighth centuries) began with the construction of a second defensive bank and ditch and ended with the abandonment of the site.

Though Dinas Powys yielded no impressive structures, the quality and quantity of imported pottery and other early Christian material from Alcock's excavations have made it possible to answer broader questions about economic and industrial aspects of British society. Dinas Powys ranks just below Tintagel and Cadbury-Congresbury in the amount of imported pottery it has yielded, which runs from the earliest imports in sub-Roman Britain to the latest. But most remarkable is the wide variety of objects that relate to industrial activity: bronze and iron metalwork, tools for jewelry-making, whetstones and querns, glass beads and other raw materials. Accompanying these were objects of likely domestic use, such as the Samian tableware, Roman and Germanic glass vessels, carved bone pins, and fine antler combs.

What has perhaps caused the most discussion is the enormous quantity of animal bones discovered at Dinas Powys. Some 12,000 bones—representing sheep, cattle, and pigs—were uncovered by the excavators, though only a fraction have been studied in detail.[258] Analyses indicate that whole animals were entering the settlement at Dinas Powys and being butchered there.[259] It is not clear, however, whether the inhabitants favored cattle or pig.

Alcock relied heavily on this information about farming economy and industry to formulate his first interpretation of Dinas Powys. He concluded that the early Christian occupation was that of a princely court (*llys*) or stronghold which received tribute in the form of food renders and whose economy depended on animal byproducts supplemented by craft industries. Although some have questioned Alcock's use of later Welsh and medieval literary sources to formulate the "*llys* model," no other interpretaion of Dinas Powys has gained acceptance. On the contrary, Alcock's model may be gaining more support as other hillfort occupation comes to light. The question, then, is how does Dinas Powys compare with other fortified sites in Wales and Dumnonia receiving imported goods in the sub-Roman period?[260] Esmonde Cleary, expressing support for Alcock's model, points out the problems presented by Dinas Powys:

> These [hillforts] ... were presumably the residences of local rulers. At Dinas Powys the artefactual assemblage included ARSW [pottery] and glass from the Rhineland, which indicates extensive contacts. The site itself was defended and therefore could presumably call upon the labor and resources of a large area round about. Yet the buildings were small and simple. Status must have been proclaimed largely by means which leave us little or no trace.[261]

The means of displaying status, if we are to judge by the evidence of Gildas and the Llandaff Charters, was likely that of clients/retainers and agricultural lands. These leave no archaeological trace, yet are arguably more valuable than lavish buildings and treasure.

DINORBEN   Probable

Description:
Hillfort

Dating Evidence:
One bronze coin of Valens (367-78)
One bronze coin of Gratian (367-75)
Late Romano-British pottery
Polychrome bead fragment
"Saxon" embossed gilt belt plate (late sixth or seventh century)

Source:
Gardner, Willoughby and H.N. Savory. *Dinorben. A Hillfort Occupied in Early Iron Age and Roman Times*. Cardiff: National Museum of Wales, 1964.

More than fifty years of excavation at the multivallate hillfort of Dinorben in Denbighshire revealed several periods of discontinuous occupation spanning the early Iron Age to the sub-Roman period. Around 260, a large roundhouse was built at the northern end of the site, followed by the construction of small curvilinear huts at the southern end.[262] Associated items include a large number of Roman coins, the latest being two very worn "House of Valentinian" bronzes from Arles.[263] By the fourth century, Dinorben appears to have become a rural estate, akin to a southern villa, with the roundhouse possibly representing the residence of a Romano-Celtic noble.[264] The roundhouse was succeeded, probably in the early fifth century, by a roughly constructed aisled timber dwelling (identified from a system of postholes) at the northern end associated with fragments of late Roman flanged bowls of fine pink ware.[265] A sub-Roman reoccupation thus seems likely, though it is not yet possible to trace the continuity between this early fifth- century community and the latest objects from the site, which include several "Anglo-Saxon" ornamental bronze items, a bronze stud (similar to those found at Dinas Powys), and a polychrome (dark blue with white zig-sag lines and yellow and green circular patches) glass bead fragment.[266]

GATEHOLM   Probable

Description:
Island settlement

Dating Evidence:
Coins of Carausius and Tetricius I
Samian and mortaria fragments (c.250-350)
Two sherds of Oxford color-coated ware (late fourth century)
A bronze stag figurine
A bronze ringed pin (sixth to ninth century)
A perforated whetstone
A shale ring

Sources:
Cantrill, T.C. "The Hut-Circles on Gateholm, Pembrokeshire." *Archaeologia Cambrensis* (1910): 271-82.
Davies, J.L. et al. "The Hut Settlement on Gateholm, Pembrokeshire." *Archaeologia Cambrensis* 120 (1971): 102-10.
Gordon Williams, J.P. "Note on a Bronze Stag from Gateholm etc." *Archaeologia Cambrensis* 81 (1926): 191.
Lane, Alan. "Gateholm." In *Early Medieval Settlements in Wales AD 400-1100*, ed. N. Edwards and A. Lane, pp. 72-75. Cardiff: Univ. of Wales Press, 1988.
Lethbridge, T.C. and H.E. David. "Excavation of a House-Site on Gateholm, Pembrokeshire." *Archaeologia Cambrensis* 85 (1930): 366-74.

Gateholm is a small tidal island in the Broad Sound which was perhaps once a promontory attached to the mainland. Its eroding cliffs lead up to a flat plateau which is covered with rows of turf-grown walls. These are seemingly the remains of several sub-rectangular buildings, organized in a more or less homogeneous plan, perhaps protected by a drystone bank. Excavations and occasional finds indicate a long span of occupation.

Activity in the Roman period is indicated by several fragments (31 sherds from 12-18 vessels) of mortaria and samian wares, spanning c.250-350, and one coin each of Carausius and Tetricius I.[267] Oxford color-coated ware suggests that activity continued to the late fourth century at least, while signs of early medieval occupation include a bronze ringed pin (of sixth- to ninth-century date) and a bronze stag (now lost), the only close parallel that has been found for the stag on the Sutton Hoo whetstone.[268]

Interpretations of the hut settlement at Gateholm have varied. Davies sees it as a homogeneous but unusual "Roman" settlement which began around 250-300 with perhaps intermittent occupation into the post-Roman period.[269] One sherd of the Oxford ware was incorporated into the cobbling of a building (seen by excavators to be one of the earlier structures) which suggests that it, at least, was not constructed until the very end of the fourth century (and possibly later).[270] Gateholm has also been compared with Tintagel and considered an isolated monastery; but reconsiderations of the nature of Tintagel have weakened this interpretation.[271]

GLAN-Y-MOR (Cold Knap)   Possible

Description:
Roman *mansio*

Dating Evidence:
Roman pottery, iron, glass, and bronze
A whetstone
A shale bracelet
Food debris yielding radiocarbon dates (600-800 and 780-1045/1155)

Sources:
Dowdell, G. "Glan-y-Mor, Barry." In *Glamorgan County History*, vol. 2, ed. H.N. Savory, pp. 344-45. Cardiff: Univ. of Wales Press, 1984.
Evans, E. et al. "A Third-Century Maritime Establishment at Cold Knap, Barry, South Glamorgan." *Britannia* 16 (1985): 57-125.
Lane, Alan. "Glan-y-Mor." In *Early Medieval Settlements in Wales AD 400-1100*, ed. N. Edwards and A. Lane, pp. 76-78. Cardiff: Univ. of Wales Press, 1988.

Excavation at Glan-y-Mor, on the Bristol Channel, revealed "an unusual Roman building complex consisting of 22 rooms and cellars divided into four ranges built around a central courtyard."[272] Signs of occupation during the Roman period include pottery, iron, glass, and bronze items. These artifacts date activity from the late first or early second century to the mid or late fourth century. The building itself probably dates to the late third century and has been identified as "a short-lived *mansio*."[273]

Subsequent to the partial demolition of this complex, a layer of rubble (containing crushed tile, charcoal, and animal bones) indicates reoccupation in possibly five of the rooms. In addition to this reoccupation, the remains of a round-cornered rectangular building (4.7m x 5.2m) were found in the southeast corner of the central courtyard. The building had a paved floor and two drains running along its walls.[274]

No definitely post-Roman artifacts were found associated with the reoccupations. However, a great quantity of food debris—including cattle, sheep, pig and dog bones; deer antlers; and limpet and periwinkle shells—were recognized "in post-Roman contexts."[275] Animal bone from one of the reoccupied rooms gave a radiocarbon date of 600-860, while other reoccupied rooms yielded a whetstone and a shale bracelet which are possibly early medieval.[276]

GRAENOG   Probable

Description:
Hut group

Dating Evidence:
Late Roman pottery (second to fourth centuries)
Remanent magnetic date of a hearth (500-550)

Sources:
Kelly, Richard S. "The Excavation of a Medieval Farmstead

at Cefn Graenog, Clynnog, Gwynedd." *BBCS* 29 (1982): 859-908.
—. "Graenog." In *Early Medieval Settlements in Wales AD 400-1100*, ed. N. Edwards and A. Lane, pp. 79-80. Cardiff: Univ. of Wales Press, 1988.
—. "Recent Research on the Hut Group Settlements of North-West Wales." In *Conquest, Co-Existence and Change*, ed. B.C. Burnham and J.L. Davies, pp. 102-11. Lampeter, Dyfed: St. David's Univ. College, 1990.

Graenog is the site of three structures which are part of a round-hut group. Sherds of plain samian pottery and Roman coarse wares have been found over most of the site, dating activity in the second through fourth centuries. After this Roman-period occupation, the structures were re-used and a corn-drying kiln was constructed.[277] A remanent magnetic date from the hearth in one of the huts yielded a date of 500-550.[278]

LONGBURY BANK (Little Hoyle)   Probable

Description:
Bank and cave settlement

Dating Evidence:
Romano-British pottery
Imported pottery (PRSW, Bi, Bii, Biv, Bmisc, D and E ware)
Merovingian glass
Radiocarbon-dated charcoal (fifth or sixth century)
Silver plate (sixth century)
Type G bronze penannular brooch (seventh century)
Chisel-cut cross (?)

Sources:
Alcock, Leslie. "Post-Roman Sherds from Longbury Bank Cave, Penally (Pembs.)." *BBCS* 18 (1958): 77-79.
Campbell, Ewan. "Longbury Bank." In *Early Medieval Settlements in Wales AD 400-1100*, ed. N. Edwards and A. Lane, pp. 88-90 and Appendix 1. Cardiff: Univ. of Wales Press, 1988.
Campbell, Ewan and Alan Lane. "Excavations at Longbury Bank, Dyfed." *Medieval Archaeology* 37 (1993): 15-77.
Green, H.S. "Excavations at Little Hoyle (Longbury Bank) Wales, in 1984." In *Studies in the Upper Paleolithic of Britain and N. W. Europe*, ed. D.A. Roe, pp. 99-119. BAR No. 296. Oxford: BAR Publishing, 1986.

Longbury Bank rests on a flat-topped limestone ridge in Pembrokeshire. Several excavations have been carried out on a small cave (Little Hoyle) which runs under the Bank, and an enigmatic vertical shaft rises to the summit of the ridge. There are no visible structures or earthworks on the summit, but a slight break in the slope running across the promontory suggests a boundary or defense.

Roman pottery was discovered in trenches cut (by modern excavators) into the Bank, and two fourth-century Roman coins were found at the nearby manor house of Trefloyne.[279] Excavations in this century and the last have produced a large quantity of sherds of imported pottery (1 PRSW dish; 1 Bi, 1 or 2 Bii, 1 Biv, and 1 or 2 Bmisc *amphorae*; a mortarium and a plate of D ware; and 5 E ware vessels), as well as a silver trapezoidal plate of possible Byzantine import, and 63 fragments from at least 15 Merovingian glass drinking vessels.[280] Items of local provenance include a Type G bronze penannular brooch, an annular loom-weight, shells from various molluscs, and animal bones (mostly cattle).[281] Two samples of charcoal, which yielded radiocarbon dates centering in the fifth or sixth centuries, confirm late Roman activity and occupation in the late fifth through seventh centuries.[282]

Due to the absence of identifiable structures, it has been difficult to interpret the early medieval settlement at Longbury Bank. Some have suggested occupation within the cave, which was possibly the retreat of a hermit from one of the nearby monasteries (Penally or Caldey).[283] A simple chisel-cut cross was found above the floor of the shaft, but its date remains problematic.[284] Most of the imported pottery was found on the summit of the bank, and the site could just as well have been a secular—possibly royal—settlement.[285] "The association with exotic food and drink is clear," write Campbell and Lane, "and the status of those people able to afford such luxuries can be assumed to be high."[286]

TY MAWR   Probable

Description:
Hut group

Dating Evidence:
Theodosian coin hoard
Uncalibrated radiocarbon dates: 520, 530, 540, and 580 ad

Sources:
Edwards, Nancy. "Ty Mawr." In *Early Medieval Settlements in Wales AD 400-1100*, ed. N. Edwards and A. Lane, pp. 118-20. Cardiff: Univ. of Wales Press, 1988.
Kelly, Richard S. "Recent Research on the Hut Group Settlements of North-West Wales." In *Conquest, Co-Existence and Change*, ed. B.C. Burnham and J.L. Davies, pp. 102-11. Lampeter, Dyfed: St. David's Univ. College, 1990.
Smith, C.A. "The Hut Circles at Holyhead Mountain: An Interim Report on Excavations in 1978 and 1979." *Archaeologia Cambrensis* 129 (1980): 151-53.
—. "Excavations at the Ty Mawr Hut-Circles, Holyhead, Anglesey, Part I." *Archaeologia Cambrensis* 133 (1984): 64-82.
—. "Excavations at the Ty Mawr Hut-Circles, Holyhead, Anglesey. Part II." *Archaeologia Cambrensis* 134 (1985): 11-52.
—. "Excavations at the Ty Mawr Hut-Circles, Anglesey: Part III: the Finds." *Archaeologia Cambrensis* 135 (1986): 12-80.
—. "Excavations at the Ty Mawr Hut-Circles, Holyhead, Anglesey, Part IV: Chronology and Discussion." *Archaeologia Cambrensis* 136 (1987): 20-38.

Ty Mawr is a large group of mostly circular stone huts situated on the southern slopes of Holyhead Mountain. The huts lay below an ancient hillfort and are associated with fields which were enclosed and cultivated by the inhabitants. Much attention has been paid to the prehistoric phase of the hut settlement. Late Roman use of the Mountain, perhaps as a naval lookout station, is suggested by traces of a signal tower and by a hoard of 22 Theodosian coins, including a clipped *siliqua* of either Arcadius or Honorius.[287] Roman pottery and third- and fourth-century coins associated with the huts were discovered by early excavators, though more recently the identification of the group as a Romano-British village has been questioned.[288]

Excavations by Christopher Smith in 1978 to 1982 strongly indicated sub-Roman occupation in the eastern part of the Ty Mawr group. Radiocarbon determinations placed two of the huts (T3 and T4) in the sixth century AD, and indicated the re-use of an older structure (T1) in this period as well as an episode of cultivation in the ancient fields.[289] Determinations from the site were taken from a large midden of shellfish (mainly limpet) and the charred remains of naked barley and spelt found in "hearths" in the sixth-century huts.[290] Though the original roundhouse may have been reoccupied, Smith noted that the two sub-Roman huts were smaller and more rectangular than the much earlier hut-circles.[291] Known locally as *Cytian'r Gwyddelod*, "the cottages (or huts) of the Goidels (or Irish)," Ty Mawr may have hosted Irish immigrants in the late or sub-Roman periods, though the name could alternatively refer to indigenous occupants.[292]

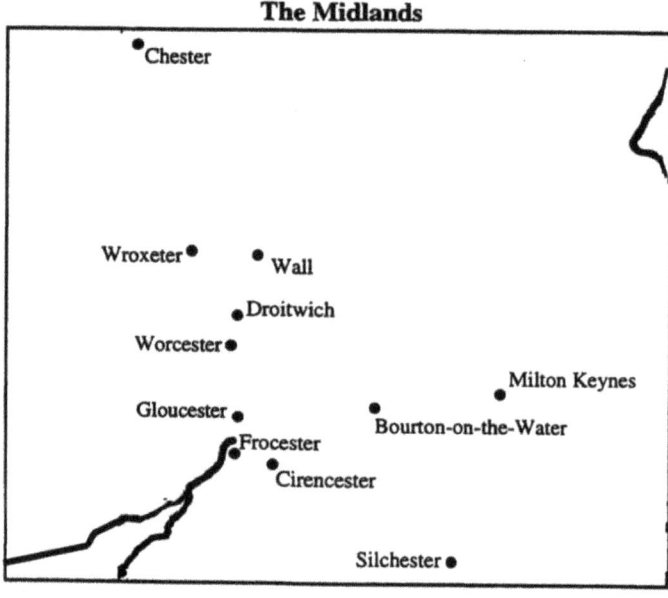

The Midlands

BOURTON-ON-THE-WATER   Possible

Description:
Small unfortified town

Dating Evidence:
One coin of Valentinian
One coin of Honorius
Merovingian (?) grey-ware pottery

Sources:
Dunning, G.C. "Salmonsbury, Bourton on the Water, Gloucestershire." In *Hillforts: Later Prehistoric Earthworks in Britain and Ireland*, ed. D.W. Harding, pp. 75-118. London: Academic Press, 1976.
O'Neil, H.E. "The Roman Settlement on the Fosse Way at Bourton Bridge, Bourton on the Water, Glos." *Transactions of the Bristol and Gloucestershire Archaeological Society* 87 (1968): 29-55.

Bourton was a thriving Roman settlement which developed near the native hillfort of Salmonsbury.[293] One excavated Roman structure yielded a coin of Valentinian sealed beneath a pavement, and a coin of Honorius was also found on the site.[294] The coins, along with a sherd of fine wheel-turned grey-ware pottery, possibly Merovingian, suggests continued activity through the fifth century.

CHESTER (*Deva*)   Definite

Description:
Legionary fortress

Dating Evidence:
Roman coinage (c.368-73)
Imported pottery (ARSW, Biv, D and E ware)
Shell-gritted pottery

Sources:
Higham, N.J. *The Origins of Cheshire*. Manchester and New York: Manchester Univ. Press, 1993.
Laing, Lloyd and Jennifer. *The Dark Ages of West Chester*. Council Monograph Series No. 6. Chester: City Council, 1986.
Mason, D.J.P. *Excavations at Chester: A Possible Roman Posting House*. Chester: City Council, 1980.
McPeake, J.C. "The End of the Affair." In *New Evidence for Roman Chester*, ed. T.J. Strickland and P.J. Davey, pp. 41-44. Liverpool: Liverpool Univ. Press, 1978.
McPeake, J.C., et al. "Excavations in the Garden of No. 1 Abbey Green, Chester, 1975-77: Interim Report." *Journal of the Chester Archaeological Society* 63 (1980): 15-37.
Strickland, T.J. "Chester." *Current Archaeology* 84 (1982): 6-12.
—. "The Roman Heritage of Chester: The Survival of the Buildings of *Deva* after the Roman Period." *Journal of the Chester Archaeological Society* 67 (1984): 17-36.
Strickland, T.J. and P.J. Davey, eds. *New Evidence for Roman Chester*. Liverpool: Liverpool Univ. Press, 1978.
Ward, Simon. *Excavations at Chester: Roman Headquarters Building to Medieval Row*. Chester: City Council, 1988.

The Roman legionary fortress at Chester was altered dramatically at the end of the third century, when its barracks were completely demolished. The Chester legion, *legio XX Valeria Victrix*, does not appear in the *Notitia Dignitatum*, and coinage inside the fortress seems to have run out about 373.[295] Recent excavation has shown, however, that the administrative buildings at the center of the fortress remained in use after the barracks were demolished and were even refurbished in the fourth century.²⁹⁶ Strickland sees fourth-century Chester as "purely an administrative centre, surrounded by acres of [paved] open space, where a field army, when it did eventually come to base, could occasionally bivouac."²⁹⁷

It is possible that this administrative role was continued by Chester even after the troop withdrawals of the early fifth century. When buildings were destroyed in the third and fourth centuries, their stone was often used for street-paving, and excavation has shown that these subsequent road surfaces (late fourth/early fifth century) were worn smooth.²⁹⁸ At the Abbey Green site, excavators uncovered a large (11m x 5m) timber-framed building constructed on drystone sleeper walls with a gravel and flagged floor.²⁹⁹ This building, aligned along the Roman street, apparently underwent several modifications in the fifth and sixth centuries datable by the presence of *amphorae* and red color-coated vessels imported from the Mediterranean. Higham sees the imported pottery as a sign that Chester's port was still in operation, with a flourishing church in the city causing a demand for wine and oil.³⁰⁰

The Laings interpret this as evidence that Chester was the sub-Roman civil administrative center of the kingdom of Powys.³⁰¹ The remains of metalworking (both iron and bronze) found at the Abbey Green site could support the theory of high-satus occupation continuing in the city.³⁰² Although, as yet, the archaeological evidence of sub-Roman occupation in Chester is sparse,³⁰³ the literary evidence amply testifies to a continuing British presence. Bede records two notable events occuring in or near the city at the turn of the seventh century. The first is a council of Welsh church leaders c.601 called in response to Augustine's demands for British obeisance.³⁰⁴ After the Britons reject the new archbishop of Canterbury, Bede records (gleefully) the destruction of a British army, along with 1200 British monks, at the Battle of Chester (*ad civitatem Legionum*) in 615.³⁰⁵ Nennius, a century later, lists Chester (*in urbe Legionis*) as the site of Arthur's ninth battle against the Saxons in the sixth century.³⁰⁶ Chester has also been suggested as the base from which St. Germanus set out to win the Alleluia Victory in 429.³⁰⁷ According to the *Anglo-Saxon Chronicle*, Chester's Roman defenses were in such good shape in the year 894 that they were used by a band of Danes to withstand a two-day siege by English levies.³⁰⁸

CIRENCESTER (*Corinium Dobunnorum*)   Probable

Description:
Civitas capital

Dating Evidence:
One *siliqua* of Honorius
Color-coated pottery (late fourth century)
Grass-tempered pottery (fifth or sixth century)

Sources:
McWhirr, Alan. *Cirencester Excavations III: Houses in Roman Cirencester*. Cirencester: Excavations Committee, 1986.
—. "Cirencester—'Corinium Dobunnorum.'" In *Roman Towns: The Wheeler Inheritance: A Review of 50 Years' Research*, ed. S.J. Greep, pp. 46-49. CBA Research Report No. 93. York: CBA, 1993.
McWhirr, A.D., ed. *Studies in the Archaeology and History of Cirencester*. BAR No. 30. Oxford: BAR Publishing, 1976.
McWhirr, Alan *et al.*, eds. *Cirencester Excavaions II: Romano-British Cemeteries at Cirencester*. Cirencester: Excavations Committee, 1982.
Reece, Richard. "From Corinion to Cirencester." In *Studies in the Archaeology and History of Cirencester*, ed. A. Mc Whirr. BAR No. 30. Oxford: BAR Publishing, 1976.
Reece, Richard and Christopher Catling. *Cirencester: The Development and Buildings of a Cotswold Town*. BAR No. 12. Oxford: BAR Publishing, 1975.
Wacher, John. "Late Roman Developments." In *Studies in the Archaeology and History of Cirencester*, ed. A. McWhirr, pp. 15-18. BAR No. 30. Oxford: BAR Publishing, 1976.

Cirencester was Roman Britain's "Second City," after London, and contained flourishing mosaic and sculpture workshops. But the evidence for late Roman Cirencester produces a mixed picture of continued occupation and decay. The floor of the forum was quite worn down, but it was also kept clean and apparently the market flourished here after the cessation of coins.³⁰⁹ The Verulamium Gate underwent the refacing of its tower, the rebuilding of the front face of the wall, and the provision of a sluice gate and other flood-prevention work which has been dated on ceramic evidence to the beginning of the fifth century.³¹⁰ A roadside ditch beside Ermine Street yielded evidence that the road also remained well-used (and often repaired), until grass began to grow on it and two unburied bodies were left to rot in the ditch.³¹¹

There is good evidence for an early Christian presence in Cirencester. As the administrative capital of the province *Britannia Prima*, Cirencester was likely the see of a bishop, and it has been suggested that the British bishop missing (but represented by a deacon) at the Council of Arles was from Cirencester.³¹² A Christian palindrome, whose letters can be rearranged to form a cross from the words PATER NOSTER, was found carefully scratched into the wall plaster of a house on Victoria Road. It clearly dates from a time when open references to Christianity would have invited persecution.³¹³ Excavations at Cirencester's urban cemeteries have yet to yield any clues about this Christian presence. Of the over 400 skeletons exhumed, most were of fourth- or early fifth-century date.³¹⁴

An accumulation of silt and debris in roadside ditches signals that Cirencester began to decline in the middle of the fifth century. At that time, the city population seems to have abandoned their old dwellings and resettled inside the town amphitheatre. In the amphitheatre, which lies just outside the city walls on the Fosse Way, there is abundant evidence of timber buildings and road and wall repairs dated, from associated coins and (grass-tempered) pottery, to the late fifth century.³¹⁵ This has been interpreted as a shrinking city population moving into a smaller and more easily defended area, perhaps to flee disease and epidemic. There is ample evidence from

Gaul and Dacia where Roman amphitheatres were converted into miniature fortified towns.[316] The *ceaster* of Chesterton, the modern district wherein the amphitheatre lies, may refer to this fortified settlement.[317]

Was it, then, the amphitheatre of Cirencester rather than the city itself that fell to the Saxons in the Battle of Dyrham in 577? Excavation has revealed no signs of violent destruction in the city. "It may be that the population of fifth century Corinium was no more than a collection of farming families," write Reece and Catling.[318]

DROITWICH (*Salinae, Saltwic*)   Probable

Description:
Small town; salt mine

Dating Evidence:
Late Roman pottery
A coin of Honorius
Radiocarbon dated charcoal (cal AD 435±95 and cal AD 630±30)
Grass-tempered wares
"Anglo-Saxon" pottery and fabrics

Sources:
Gelling, P.S. "Report on Excavation in Bay's Meadow, Droitwich 1954-55." *Transactions of the Birmingham Archaeological Society* 75 (1957): 1-23.
Hurst, Derek. "Major Saxon Discoveries at Droitwich." *Current Archaeology* 126 (1991): 252-55.

Droitwich began as a Roman fort established to supervise salt mining at the local brine springs.[319] One late Roman aisled house contained a paving which sealed a coin of Honorius.[320] Traces of timber frame buildings also support the view of post-Roman activity continuing at the town, while mining activity certainly continued into the Anglo-Saxon period. At the Upwich Pit, a series of ten brine-boiling hearths and several stake alignments were contructed, the hearths still containing ash and charcoal residue from the processing of salt through this brine-boiling method.[321] Radiocarbon determinations from the charcoal residues provided dates of between cal AD 435±95 and cal AD 630±30. Sub-Roman to Anglo-Saxon continuity seems likely from the presence of an assemblage of grass-tempered wares, pagan "Anglo-Saxon" stamp-decorated pottery, and fragments of "Anglo-Saxon" fabrics. References to *Saltwic* are found throughout middle and late Saxon charters.

FROCESTER   Possible

Description:
Villas

Dating Evidence:
Grass-tempered pottery

Source:
Heighway, Carolyn. *Anglo-Saxon Gloucestershire*. Gloucester: Sutton, 1987.

Two Roman villas at Frocester have produced fifth-century burials, with one of these—Frocester Court villa—producing evidence of sub-Roman timber structures.[322] The stone buildings at Frocester Court were inhabited until the end of the fourth century, though one room had been converted into a stable. In the early fifth century, the villa residents abandoned the stone house and erected at least two timber structures in the courtyard. One building, 14m x 3m, appears to have been a hall built on sill beams laid flat (no postholes were found) on a floor of stone and gravel. Around this building and in and under its floor were dozens of sherds of grass-tempered pottery. A second structure, 12m x 9m, was erected across part of the courtyard hall and defined by a timber beam-slot and internal postholes. Four graves found in the courtyard have also been identified as fifth-century burials. Heighway sees Frocester as a significant fifth-century center in Gloucestershire, "perhaps a rural market."[323]

GLOUCESTER (*Glevum*)   Definite

Description:
Colonia

Dating Evidence:
Fel. Temp. Reparatio immitation coins (c.350-75)
12 coins of Honorius
29 coins of Arcadius
Shell-tempered and Oxfordshire wares (late fourth century)
Radiocarbon-dated timber (AD 430±80)
Imported pottery (Bv)
One penannular brooch

Sources:
Bryant, R. "Excavations at the Church of St. Mary de Lode, Gloucester." *Bulletin of the CBA Churches Committee* 13 (1980): 15-18.
Heighway, Carolyn. *Anglo-Saxon Gloucestershire*. Gloucester: Sutton, 1987.
Heighway, C.M. *et al.* "Excavations at 1 Westgate Street, Gloucester." *Medieval Archaeology* 23 (1979): 159-213.
Hurst, H.R. *Gloucester, the Roman and Later Defenses*. Gloucester: Archaeological Publications, 1986.
—. "Excavations at Gloucester, 1968-71." *Antiquaries Journal* 52 (1972): 24-69.
—. "Excavations at Gloucester, 1971-3, Second Interim Report, Part II." *Antiquaries Journal* 54 (1974): 8-52.
—. "Excavations at Gloucester, Third Interim Report: Kingsholm, 1965-75." *Antiquaries Journal* 55 (1975): 267-94.

The military presence in Gloucester in the years leading up to 400 seems to have been very high. The late Roman walling of the city was likely part of a scheme to fortify all the major settlements along the tributaries of the Severn River, to control Irish or Saxon raids up the Bristol Channel.[324] Gloucester's forum area was in continuous use after the forum itself had been dismantled in the late fourth century, with timber structures replacing stone and evidence of re-planning in the town center in the early fifth century.[325]

Coin evidence associated with the last phase of metalling indicates that the whole forum may have been resurfaced after 390.[326] A colonnaded stone stucture near the forum was demolished c.370, only to be replaced by a timber building which yielded a radiocarbon date of AD 430±80.[327] The new timber structure may have been a sub-Roman market booth, for it contained a quantity of butcher's bones. Elswhere, a coin hoard, with several coins of Honorius and Arcadius, seems to have fallen from the rafters of one building and lay on top of debris.[328] Two or three subsequent occupations overlay the deposition of *Fel. Temp. Reparatio* imitation coins on Berkeley Street.[329] A coin of Valens (364-78) was found **beneath** a mosaic on Southgate Street.[330] Ornamental metalwork, shell-tempered and Oxfordshire wares, and imported pottery (fragments of North African *amphorae*) testify to occupation continuing into at least the late fifth century.[331]

A late or post-Roman cemetery at Kingsholm may tell us more about this community.[332] That there were Christians in this community is indicated by a sub-Roman timber mausoleum, containing the skeleton of a male with silver belt-fittings, found overlying a Roman building and beneath the Saxon chapel of St. Mary de Lode.[333] According to the *Anglo-Saxon Chronicle*, Gloucester fell to the Saxons at the Battle of Dyrham in 577. If this entry is accurate, the city was then under the control of a king named Conmail. The late Roman earthwork defenses which surrounded the city would have made it an attractive residence for a sub-Roman king.[334]

MILTON KEYNES   Possible

Description:
Villa; *vicus*

Dating Evidence:
Coins of Arcadius (383-408)
Late Roman pottery
Early Saxon pottery

Sources:
Marney, P.T. *Roman and Belgic Pottery from Excavations in Milton Keynes 1972-82*. Buckinghamshire Archaeological Society, 1989.
Zeepvat, R.J. *et al. Roman Milton Keynes*. Aylesbury: Buckinghamshire Archaeological Society, 1987.

In the Milton Keynes area, both the rural site of Bancroft and the *vicus* at Dropshort (*Magiovinium*) have produced coins of Arcadius.[335] At Bancroft, late Roman and early Saxon pottery overlap each other in the same assemblage.[336]

SILCHESTER (*Calleva Atrebatum*)   Definite

Description:
Civitas capital

Dating Evidence:
700 Theodosian coins
A hoard of 51 silver *siliquae* down to Honorius
One *siliqua* of Constantine III (407-11)
Argonne sigillata pottery (c.395-420)
One North African red-surfaced pottery lamp (c.395-420)
Two penannular brooches (fourth/fifth century)
Gallo-Roman glass (fifth century)
A "Saxon" bronze button brooch (seventh century)
Ogom inscribed tombstone (seventh century)

Sources:
Boon, George C. "The Latest Objects from Silchester, Hampshire." *Medieval Archaeology* 3 (1959): 79-88.
—. *Silchester: The Roman Town of Calleva*. London: David and Charles, 1974.
—. *The Roman Town 'Calleva Atrebatum' at Silchester, Hampshire*. Reading: Calleva Museum, 1983.
Frere, S.S. *et al.* "Roman Britain in 1987." *Britannia* 19 (1988): 416-84 (477).
Fulford, Michael. *The Silchester Amphitheatre: Excavations of 1979-85*. Britannia Monograph Series No. 10. London: Society for the Promotion of Roman Studies, 1989.
—. "Excavations on the Sites of the Amphitheatre and Forum-Basilica at Silchester, Hampshire: an Interim Report." *Antiquaries Journal* 65 (1985): 39-81.
—. *Guide to the Silchester Excavations: The Forum Basilica 1982-84*. Reading: Univ. of Reading Press, 1985.
—. *Silchester Defenses 1974-80*. Britannia Monograph Series No. 5. London: Society for the Promotion of Roman Studies, 1984.
—. "Silchester." *Current Archaeology* 82 (1982): 326-31.

Silchester is one of the few former Roman cities in Britain that did not evolve into a medieval and modern town. Thus, the circuit of its Roman walls survives almost completely intact, and excavation of the now-vacant interior has revealed the most complete plan of any Roman town in Britain. The undisturbed nature of *Calleva*'s remains gives hope, as well, that we may learn more about the nature and survival of such towns in the fifth and sixth centuries.

There are numerous signs of new structures and activity in fourth-century Silchester, though the character of occupation was perhaps changing. By 300 the basilica ceased to be used as a public building, being divided by partitions and reorganized as a metal workshop.[337] As late as 320, large-scale renovations were taking place at the baths, while numerous Theodosian coins (including a bronze coin of Arcadius, c.395-402) attest to activity at the forum.[338] Sometime during the fourth century the walls of the amphitheatre were torn down, while the inn and one of the temples contained coins of Valens (364-78).[339] Some of Silchester's townhouses were given fourth-century mosaics (associated coins run down to Honorius), while the southeast gate "was deliberately blocked in the Roman or sub-Roman period" to more easily control traffic moving in and out of the city.[340] An unusually large number of very worn late Roman coins (including a *siliqua* of Constantine III, c.407-11), a North African ceramic lamp (c.395-420), fragments from late Roman glass vessels, and bronze accessories (pins, buckles, a bracelet) signify economic activity continuing at Silchester for much of the fifth century.[341]

The most interesting fourth-century structure at Silchester is the "basilican church" discovered near the forum in 1892.[342] This very small building (13m x 9m) has been the focus of much attention, not least because it was the first Roman structure in Britain to be convincingly identified as a Christian church. The identification is based on the building's plan, which is similar to Old St. Peter's in Rome, and the discovery of a "baptismal font" (a square foundation of tiles and flint-lined pit) near the main entrance.[343] No significant dating evidence (apart from some third-century pottery sealed beneath the floor) was found during the 1892 and 1961 excavations, though the plan suggests a late fourth-century erection and some later reconstruction.[344] Only a few Christian objects have been found at Silchester, and none in direct association with the basilica. The Christian community, such as it was, must have been small, though the proximity of the church to the Forum suggests that they were not without influence.

If we look at the material evidence for the fifth and sixth centuries in Silchester, apart from the Roman structures, we see a noticeably "Celtic" element asserting itself. In addition to Roman metalwork of late fourth- or early fifth-century date, there is a relative abundance of evidence of pins and penannular brooches whose affinities are Irish and Scottish. Along with this evidence there was found, in a Roman well, a tombstone inscribed with Ogom characters commemorating one EBICATOS in Irish text.[345] This figure has been seen as an Irish pilgrim or mercenary, and his tombstone has been assigned various dates from c.450 to 700.[346] It is by far the most easterly find of an Ogom inscription in Britain, and contrasts with the early Saxon material found at nearby towns like Winchester and Dorchester-on-Thames. The few Saxon finds from Silchester belong to the seventh century and later.[347]

Fitting into the notion that Silchester was a "Saxon-free zone" during the fifth and sixth centuries is a series of dykes which surround the town, the most substantial of the earthworks known as Grim's Bank. It was first proposed that Grim's Bank was constructed after the battle of Badon Hill (c.500) as a boundary between Briton and Saxon lands. This view has now been altered a bit, some now preferring a date of c.450 and seeing the dykes as the boundary of a British kingdom—a sub-Roman *civitas* of sorts—centered around Silchester.[348] This "*civitas*" likely survived as a center of British power up to the seventh century, when there begins to appear an abundance of Saxon finds in the area. There are, it should be noted, no signs of widespread destruction at *Calleva* itself.[349] Silchester's transition from British to Saxon control appears to have been both late and non-traumatic.

WALL (*Letocetum, Cair Luitcoyt*)   Possible

Description:
Small fortified town

Dating Evidence:
Coins down to Valens (364-78)

Sources:
Ball, F. and N. "Wall, Staffordshire. Roman Features at SK 096 065." *West Midlands Archaeology* 24 (1981): 118-19.

Basset, Steven. "Church and Diocese in the West Midlands: The Transition from British to Anglo-Saxon Control." In *Pastoral Care Before the Parish*, ed. J. Blair and R. Sharpe, pp. 13-40. Leicester: Leicester Univ. Press, 1992.

Crickmore, J. *Romano-British Urban Settlements in the West Midlands*. BAR British Series No. 127. Oxford: BAR Publishing, 1984.

Webster, Graham. "A Roman System of Fortified Posts along Watling Street, Britain." In *Roman Frontier Studies 1967*, ed. S. Applebaum, pp. 38-45. Tel Aviv: Univ. of Tel Aviv Press, 1971.

—. *Wall Roman Site*. London: English Heritage, 1985.

The small fortified town at Wall, in Staffordshire, is one of five situated along Watling Street forming what was likely a chain of posting stations along the Welsh frontier.[350] Coinage from stray finds and excavations runs down to the end of Roman occupation, and a single bronze bowl bearing a *Chi-Rho* monogram suggests possible Christian activity.[351] Although no fifth-century artifacts have been found at Wall, there is some literary evidence for sub-Roman occupation. Gildas mentions that there were twenty-eight cities in sub-Roman Britain without listing them; Nennius does list them, and includes Wall (*Cair Luitcoyt*) among the likes of London and Dumbarton.[352] Nennius (or the original compiler), thought to have been writing in Wales in the ninth century, is probably listing ancient settlements thought to have been important—or whose names were still known—in his day.[353] This is verified by a mention of a pagan raid on Wall (*Caer Luydcoed*) in an early Welsh poem called *Marwnad Cynddylan* ("The Lament of Cynddylan").[354] Shown to date from the seventh century, the poem describes a raid in which neither the bishop nor "the book-holding monks" were spared, suggesting the presence of an organized Christian community in Wall at that date.[355]

WORCESTER   Probable

Description:
Small town

Dating Evidence:
Fourth-century pottery
Radiocarbon dates (AD 536 and AD 585)

Sources:
Baker, Nigel. "Churches, Parishes and Early Medieval Topography." In *Medieval Worcester. An Archaeological Framework*, ed. M. Carver, *Trans. Worcester Arch. Soc.* 3rd ser., no. 7 (1980): 31-38.

Barker, P.A. *et al.* "Two Burials Under the Refectory at Worcester Cathedral." *Medieval Archaeology* 18 (1974): 146-51.

Bassett, Steven. "Churches in Worcester Before and After the Conversion of the Anglo-Saxons." *Antiquaries Journal* 69 (1989): 225-56.

Not much is know about the Roman small town of Worcester. The only Roman structure identified at Worcester is a circular building thought to be a temple or shrine, while traces of timber-framed buildings have been excavated in nearby Sidbury. The only traces of the town's fortifications are northern and eastern sections of a ditch which originally formed a circuit. It seems likely that some form of these defenses must have been standing when the Saxons arrived for them to have named their settlement *Weogorncéaster*, "Roman walled town of the people called *Weogòra*."[356]

Worcester has produced some fourth-century coins and pottery and unbroken glass vessels. Under the refectory of the Norman cathedral lay two burials probably belonging to the sub-Roman period.[357] Grave one contained a skeleton of a man (age 25-30), fragments of very fine spun gold (around the skeleton's neck), a few sherds of Roman pottery, and a single posthole. The bones yielded (uncalibrated) radiocarbon dates of AD 536 (429-643) and AD 585 (483-687). The gold thread was woven into a brocade, probably the border of a cloth garment, perhaps a priest's hood or collar. Bassett has shown (through charter evidence) that St. Helen's parish church also originated as a Roman or British church before it became the property of Hwiccan rulers and, subsequently, an Anglo-Saxon see (c.680).[358] Hwiccan conversions before (and possibly leading to) the creation of the see would then have been the work of British Christians in and around Worcester.

WROXETER (*Viroconium Cornoviorum*)   Definite

Description:
Civitas capital

Dating Evidence:
Six *plumbatae* weapons (late fourth century)
Two coins of the House of Valentinian
Two Theodosian coins of c.388-92
One coin (?) of c.395-402
One bronze coin of Valentinian III (c.430-35)
Imported Gaza amphoras (Bvi)
Inscribed memorial stone (late fifth century)
Radiocarbon-dated skeleton (AD 610±50)

Sources:
Atkinson, Donald. *Report on Excavations at Wroxeter*. Oxford: Oxford Univ. Press, 1942.
Barker, P.A. "Excavations at the Baths Basilica at Wroxeter 1966-74: Interim Report." *Britannia* 6 (1975): 106-17.
Barker, Philip, ed. *From Roman 'Viroconium' to Medieval Wroxeter*. Worcester: West Mercian Archaeological Consultants, Ltd., 1990.
Crickmore, J. *Romano-British Urban Settlements in the West Midlands*. BAR British Series No. 127. Oxford: BAR Publishing, 1984.
Gelling, Margaret. *The West Midlands in the Early Middle Ages*. Leicester: Leicester Univ. Press, 1992.
Webster, Graham. *The Cornovii*. London: Duckworth, 1975.
—. "Wroxeter (Viroconium)." In *Fortress into City*, ed. G. Webster, pp. 120-44. London: Batsford, 1988.
Webster, Graham and Philip Barker. *Wroxeter Roman City*. London: English Heritage, 1991.

White, Roger. "Excavations on the Site of the Baths Basilica." In *From Roman 'Viroconium' to Medieval Wroxeter*, ed. P. Barker, pp. 3-7. Worcester: West Mercian Archaeological Consultants, Ltd., 1990.

Wroxeter is the Roman site that has yielded the most archaeological evidence for occupation and activity during the sub-Roman period. Philip Barker's meticulous excavations have revealed, in detail, the phases of repair and reconstruction which made Wroxeter a thriving city in the fifth century while its fellow cities were in sharp decline.

After the Roman conquest, the Cornovii seem to have given up their local hillfort, the Wrekin, and moved in or near the town growing around the former legionary base at Wroxeter. It was not until after Hadrian's visit to Britain that funds were sufficient to build a forum and basilica, but slowly Wroxeter grew into a prosperous *civitas* capital. Though Wroxeter no longer quartered a legion, the Cornovii continued to raise a militia on their own—some of which was absorbed into the regular army as *Coh. I Cornoviorum*—showing an ability to protect themselves and their town.[359]

Decline appears to have set in at the beginning of the fourth century, when the forum was destroyed and the main baths suite went out of use (though the *frigidarium* quite possibly continued to be used).[360] The forum was still used as an open market, but civil activity gradually moved to the basilica in the baths complex. This building had been refloored in the late third century, repaired, then refloored three more times up to 375.[361] At this point it ceased to have a public function, and instead was turned into an industrial complex with ramshackle buildings, pits, and a furnace constructed in the interior. Again the floor showed wear, and associated coins date this activity to c.388-92.

The builder's yard did not last long, however, for it too seems to have been cleared by about 402. At this time the basilica's roof and clerestorey were carefully removed, along with all interior walls and columns, leaving an empty shell. The pits in the floor were filled and some of the tile was used to make a path, presumably to give pedestrians safe passageway through the area.[362] This phase appears to have lasted only a short while after the coin series ends.[363]

For most cities of Roman Britain, this would have been the last evidence of the final chapter of occupation. But at Wroxeter, remarkably, we have evidence that construction resumed in this period, in not one but two subsequent phases. The middle of the fifth century witnessed a major redevelopment on this site, most accurately described by the excavators themselves:

Much of the north wall of the basilica was demolished and dug out in places to well below floor level, and tons of rubble were laid down as building platforms.... It formed the foundation for a large timber-framed two-storied winged house, perhaps with towers, a verandah and central portico.... The building covered about half of the nave and stretched [to about 125 feet long and 52 feet wide].... On its western side, a long thin mortar and rubble platform marked a second building, [extending about 80 feet], which appears to have been something like a *loggia*: solid-walled on the north side and columned on the south. To the east... a substantial smaller building was put up against the eastern wall of the basilica. Its structure was most unusual for this phase in that it was built of mortared stone.... On the western side [of the former south aisle], five regular platforms of rubble 8m x 2.5m ... carried buildings leaning against the south wall of the basilica ... but the rest of the aisle was clear of any buildings leaving the entrance to the *frigidarium* accessible.... One possible use [of the *frigidarium*] might have been as a small church or chapel or, since some charred grain was found in this room ... it may have been used as a granary....

On the western portico, a series of buildings was constructed around the main doorway.... Each of these buildings was reconstructed several times during the lifetime of [the timber hall]. A further building was constructed at the junction of the west and north porticos.

The east-west street now saw some remarkable, if not unique, modifications.... Both ends of this 'gravel street' were revetted and had ramps or steps to provide pedestrian access.... North of the gravel street, the southern frontage ... was covered by a range of timber buildings which seem to have been either shops or residences. Some were placed long side onto the street, others had impressive porticoed facades. Nearly all were rebuilt at least once....[364]

These impressive structures have been described as "the last classically inspired buildings in Britain" until the eighteenth century.[365] But their interpretation is difficult. Though the complex has "the hallmarks of Roman public works, only constructed with timber,"[366] the excavators see it more as a villa than a public building, perhaps the residence of a *tyrannus* like Vortigern.[367] "Thus we have [at Wroxeter] a powerful character," agrees Webster, "building himself a kind of country mansion in the middle of the city, surrounded with small buildings, which are either stables or ... houses for his retainers."[368] Philip Dixon, however, sees part of the complex as incorporating "a covered street, similar to a shopping mall."[369]

After an unknown period of use, these elaborate structures were deliberately dismantled and removed and two smaller buildings were constructed at the western end of the basilica. The excavators have suggested 550 for this construction, though no strictly datable materials were found.[370] Finally, an inhumation burial was dug into the now-abandoned area just south of one of the buildings. Radiocarbon dating of the remains has yielded a date of 610±60.[371]

Associated coinage gives a *terminus post quem* of c.375-402 for the early phases of construction, while the radio-carbon determinations give a date of around 600 for the possible abandonment of the site.[372] But can we be more precise about the dating of the extensive rebuilding in the middle phase? A single find of imported pottery, an amphora (probably carrying wine) from Gaza, links Wroxeter with similar finds at London and Cadbury-Congresbury, but a late fifth- or early sixth-century date is the only one yet being offered.[373] Most intriguing of all is the memorial stone, whose inscription commemorates an Irishman named *Cunorix*, found just outside the Wroxeter defenses.[374] Kenneth Jackson dated the inscription to the late fifth century, and many have seen this Cunorix as an Irish mercenery hired to protect the city.[375]

The North

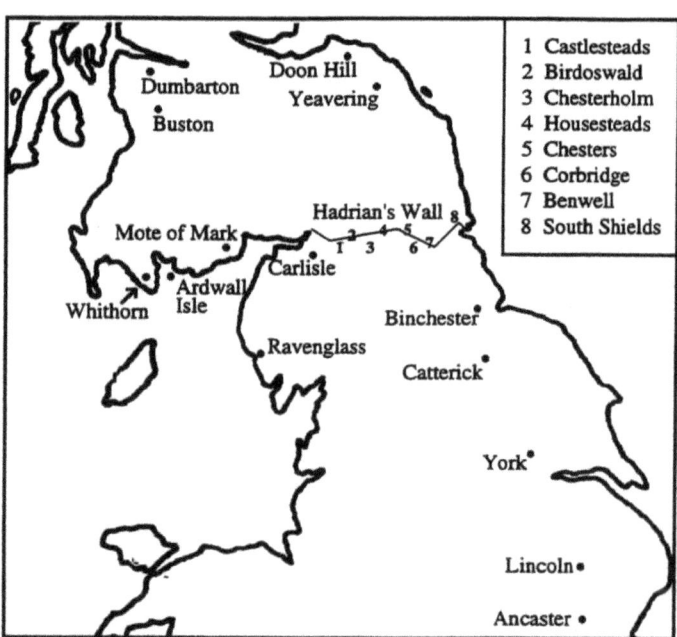

1 Castlesteads
2 Birdoswald
3 Chesterholm
4 Housesteads
5 Chesters
6 Corbridge
7 Benwell
8 South Shields

ANCASTER   Possible

Description:
Roman fort and *vicus*

Dating Evidence:
Late Roman pottery
40 "Anglo-Saxon" cremation urns (c.450)

Sources:
Todd, Malcolm. *The Roman Town of Ancaster*. Exeter: Exeter Univ. Press, 1981.
Wilson, D.M. "An Early Christian Cemetery at Ancaster." In *Christianity in Britain 300-700*, ed. M.W. Barley and R.P.C. Hanson, pp. 197-200. Leicester: Leicester Univ. Press, 1968.

A *vicus* or small town developed alongside the Roman fort at Ancaster, but the character of that settlement is not clear. Outside of the defenses, to the west, excavators uncovered a late Roman cemetery containing over 300 inhumations. Most were stone-lined graves or wooden coffins aligned east-west, and few contained associated grave-goods, leading some to speculate that this was a Christian cemetery.[376] Coins found in one grave date to the 360s, but it is possible that the burials continue into the fifth century.[377] Though no artifacts of this period identified as "Anglo-Saxon" have been found within the town, a cemetery to the southeast has yielded 40 cremation urns, common in pagan Saxon cemeteries.[378]

ARDWALL ISLE   Possible

Description:
Early Christian site

Dating Evidence:
Cross-incised slabs

Source:
Thomas, Charles. "An Early Christian Cemetery and Chapel in Ardwall Isle, Kircudbright." *Medieval Archaeology* 11 (1967): 127-88.

Excavations at Ardwall Isle, off the Kircudbright coast, have revealed significant evidence of an early medieval Christian community. Thomas has assigned the early medieval activity to three phases.[379] Phase I, which is thought to have begun in the late fifth century, describes an unenclosed cemetery with inhumations surrounding a small rock-cut hollow (identified by Thomas as the bottom of a "slab-shrine"). During Phase II, perhaps in the seventh century, this cemetery was succeeded by another, whose graves were aligned on the axis of a "corner-post" shrine, with postholes perhaps representing a timber oratory or chapel. Grave-markers accompanying the Phase II burials included slabs with incised crosses and what appears to be a portable stone altar.[380] Phase III saw further aligned burials and a stone chapel and hut. Thomas interprets much of this evidence as a sign of increasing Irish influence in the area.[381]

BINCHESTER (*Vinovia/Vinovium*) Possible

Description:
Roman fort and *vicus*

Dating Evidence:
Crambeck Ware

Sources:
Dark, K.R. "A Sub-Roman Re-Defense of Hadrian's Wall?" *Britannia* 23 (1992): 111-20.
Ferris, I.M. and R.F.J. "Excavations at Binchester 1976-9." In *Roman Frontier Studies 1979*, ed. W.S. Hanson and L.J.F. Keppie, pp. 233-54. BAR International Series No. 71. Oxford: BAR Publishing, 1980.
Welsby, Derek A. *The Roman Military Defense of the British Provinces in its Later Phases*. BAR British Series No. 101. Oxford: BAR Publishing, 1982.

At Binchester, a fort just south of Hadrian's Wall, occupation continued after the introduction of the latest coins (of Magnentius, 350-53) and of pottery from the Crambeck kilns (conventionally dated post-370).[382] The *praetorium* had an undisturbed rubbish deposit in its yard, suggesting that it decayed naturally and was possibly in use in the fifth century.[383] But there was a change in the character of occupation during this period, as military buildings were put to non-military purposes. By the sixth century, "Anglo-Saxon" burials and artifacts begin to appear.[384]

BUSTON/BUISTON Possible

Description:
Crannog

Dating Evidence:
Radiocarbon samples (370±50 ad and 520±50 ad)

Source:
Crone, Anne. "Buiston Crannog." *Current Archaeology* 127 (1991): 295-97.

This native dwelling showed signs of occupation in both the Roman early medieval periods, with several alterations spanning that time. Radiocarbon samples taken from timber stakes yielded dates of 370±50 ad and 520±50 ad.[385] Decorated wooden objects were preserved in a slumped hollow between the fifth-century house and its seventh-century framework.

CARLISLE (*Luguvalium*) Probable

Description:
Civitas capital

Dating Evidence:
A *solidus* of Valentinian II (c.388-92)
A coin of Arcadius

Sources:
Higham, Nicholas and Barri Jones. *The Carvetii*. Gloucester: Sutton, 1985.
Keevill, G.D. *et al.* "A Solidus of Valentinian II from Scotch Street, Carlisle." *Britannia* 20 (1989): 254-55.
McCarthy, M.R. "Thomas, Chadwick and Post-Roman Carlisle." In *The Early Church in Western Britain and Ireland*, ed. S.M. Pearce, pp. 241-56. BAR No. 102. Oxford: BAR Publishing, 1982.
—. *A Roman, Anglian and Medieval Site at Blackfriars Street*. Kendal, Cumbria: Cumberland and Westmorland Antiquarian and Archaeological Society, 1990.
McCarthy, Mike *et al.* "Carlisle." *Current Archaeology* 116 (1989): 298-302.
Selkirk, Andrew. "Carlisle." *Current Archaeology* 101 (1986): 172-77.

Carlisle was elevated to the status of *civitas* capital rather late, perhaps by Caracalla in the third century. By the fourth century, Carlisle was part of the defense system of Hadrian's Wall, possibly even its headquarters.[386] Although excavation has not been extensive here, Carlisle does show some signs of sub-Roman occupation. Excavation at Blackfriars Street revealed two Roman masonry buildings that were reconstructed in timber and occupied into the early fifth century.[387] After a time these were abandoned and replaced by one "large hall-like building ... constructed on a completely different alignment, which even ignored the Roman street lines."[388] At Scotch Street, excavators uncovered a large townhouse, complete with under-floor heating, that was constructed in the last quarter of the fourth century.[389] Though the hypocaust went out of use by the beginning of the fifth century,[390] the building showed signs of continued use and wear.[391] There is slim evidence of sixth-century occupation, however, despite the fact that Carlisle has long been thought to have been the administrative center of the British kingdom of Rheged.[392]

Christianity may provide the evidence bridging the gap between the Roman and sub-Roman communities in Carlisle. Evidence of an early Christian community consists only of a tombstone and a gold ring with an incised palm branch; but Thomas has argued that, as a *civitas* capital, Carlisle must have also been a bishopric, and perhaps the bishopric of the British saints Ninian and Patrick.³⁹³ When St. Cuthbert visited Carlisle in the seventh century, he was greeted by a man described as *praepositus civitatis*, and was able to walk along the town walls and see a working fountain (implying that there was still a functioning aqueduct in the city).³⁹⁴ Burnham and Wacher point out that these are strong signs of continuity: "In this way the Church, as in many other parts of the western empire, would have formed the bridge by which a moderately civilized Romano-British community was maintained and eventually transformed into an English one."³⁹⁵

CATTERICK (*Cataractonium, Catraeth*) Probable

Description:
Roman fort and *vicus*; possible battle site

Dating Evidence:
Two late Roman military buckles and a buckle-plate
"Anglo-Saxon" pottery (late fifth or early sixth century)

Sources:
Alcock, Leslie. "Gwyr y Gogledd: An Archaeological Appraisal." *Archaeologia Cambrensis* 132 (1984): 1-18.
Faull, Margaret L. "Settlement and Society in North-East England in the Fifth Century." In *Settlement and Society in the Roman North*, ed. P.R. Wilson *et al.*, pp. 49-52. Bradford, West Yorkshire: Yorkshire Archaeological Society, 1984.
Hartley, B.R. and R. Leon Fitts. *The Brigantes*. Gloucester: Sutton, 1988.
Wilson, P.R. "Recent Work at Catterick." In *Settlement and Society in the Roman North*, ed. P.R. Wilson *et al.*, pp. 75-82. Bradford, West Yorkshire: Yorkshire Archaeological Society, 1984.

The *vicus* which grew up inside the Roman fortress at Catterick shows strong signs of continued occupation in the fifth century. One building was altered in the last decades of the fourth century, when an apse was added to its west end. "This apsidial building remained in use long enough for occupation material to collect on its floors," write Burnham and Wacher, "after which it fell into decay, with soil accumulating around its walls and over its floor."³⁹⁶ Some time later a timber-framed house was built on top of the earlier stone building, its walls on a different alignment, which must (on stratigraphic grounds) be attributed to the fifth century. Other timber structures share similar structural features and would appear to be of the same phase.³⁹⁷

It would appear that a substantial Romano-British settlement still existed at Catterick," write Burnham and Wacher, "sheltered by its massive walls, at least in the first part of the century...."³⁹⁸ But can we extend this "Romano-British" occupation to the late sixth century and the Battle of Catraeth? The poems of Taliesin seem to equate Catterick with Catraeth, the seat of King Urien of Rheged and the destination of the warriors in the *Gododdin* of Aneirin.³⁹⁹ Alcock has questioned this identification, pointing out the early Saxon material (a *Grubenhäus*, pottery, brooches, and assorted military items) found in and around the *vicus*, which has produced no identifiable "British" items of the sixth and later centuries.⁴⁰⁰ While both Alcock and Wacher agree that Catterick is most likely the site of the Battle of Catraeth, it is less clear when this settlement finally came into Anglian hands.

DOON HILL Possible

Description:
Palisaded enclosure

Sources:
Alcock, Leslie. "Gwyr y Gogledd: An Archaeological Appraisal." *Archaeologia Cambrensis* 132 (1983): 1-14.
Hope-Taylor, Brian. "Balbridie ... and Doon Hill." *Current Archaeology* 72 (1980): 18-19.
Reynolds, Nicholas. "Dark Age Timber Halls and the Background to Excavation at Balbridie." *Scottish Archaeological Forum* 10 (1980): 41-60.

Doon Hill is the site of the only completely excavated plan of a northern British Hall. Within a polygonal palisaded enclosure lies Hall A, a massive rectangular timber building (70 ft. x 32 ft.) with slightly tapering end bays, two central doors, and the lateral division of a central hall with private apartments at each end.⁴⁰¹ It parallels both the large hall at South Cadbury and another northern British hall at Balbridie.⁴⁰² "Doon Hill A was certainly an impressive building," writes Alcock, "and taking account of the surrounding palisade, we should see it, in British terms, as a princely *neuadd* [hall] set within the appropriate *llys* [court]."⁴⁰³

"Doon Hill might be representative of an archetypal British form," adds Hope-Taylor, "from which 'Yeavering-style' building could directly have been developed, ... a product of the sixth or possibly the fifth century AD."⁴⁰⁴ But there seems to be a bit of confusion concerning the date of Doon Hill Hall A. It was superseded by a second hall—Hall B—which was built according to a different plan, one which more closely resembles the hall at Yeavering. The Yeavering hall has been dated c.640, so Doon Hill Hall A must have been built prior to this time, before the Angles reached *Din Eidyn* (Edinburgh) in 638.⁴⁰⁵ It appears that Doon Hill represents, like Yeavering, a British stronghold taken over by Anglian expansion in the seventh century.⁴⁰⁶

DUMBARTON ROCK (*Alt Clut/Alcluith*) Definite

Description:
Hillfort

Dating Evidence:
Imported pottery (Bi, Bii, and E ware)
Glass and metalwork (fifth/sixth century)
Radiocarbon dates (sixth century?)

Sources:
Alcock, Leslie. "A Multi-Disciplinary Chronology for Alt

Clut, Castle Rock, Dumbarton." *PSAS* 107 (1976): 103-13.

—. "The North Britons, the Picts and the Scots." In *The End of Roman Britain*, ed. P.J. Casey, pp. 134-42. BAR British Series No. 71. Oxford: BAR Publishing, 1979.

—. "Gwyr y Gogledd: An Archaeological Appraisal." *Archaeologia Cambrensis* 132 (1983): 1-18.

—. "The Activities of Potentates in Celtic Britain, AD 500-800: A Positivist Approach." In *Power and Politics in Early Medieval Britain and Ireland*, ed. S.T. Driscoll and M.R. Nieke, pp. 22-46. Edinburgh: Edinburgh Univ. Press, 1988.

Castle Rock, Dumbarton—*Alt Clut* in the British tongue—lies on the north shore of the River Clyde in the heart of the British kingdom of Strathclyde. Bede calls it both *urbs* and *civitas Brettonum munitissima*, and Adomnan insists that King Roderc of Strathclyde "ruled on Clyde Rock."[407] With its twin summits and picturesque castle, there has been much speculation about this craggy citadel.

Leslie Alcock's excavations at Dumbarton in 1974 and 1975 revealed no coherent defensive plan, but an area on the eastern spur revealed exciting evidence of sub-Roman occupation. There were the remains of "a dry-stone terrace or fighting platform, laced and revetted with timber beams."[408] Radiocarbon estimates from the oak timbers of the terrace suggest either that it had been built in the sixth century and repaired in the seventh, or that it was a work entirely of the seventh century.[409] Like the ramparts at the Mote of Mark, this structure too was destroyed by fire, probably as a result of a Viking siege in the ninth century.[410]

The artifactual evidence from Dumbarton, however, points to a fifth- and sixth-century date for the occupation. Finds include sherds of *amphorae* from the eastern Aegean and southwest Asia Minor (probably containing wine), Gaulish kitchenware, Merovingian glass, and jewelry-making debris.[411] "This [evidence] points clearly to Alt Clut as one of the dynastic centres of Strathclyde by the time of Rhydderch [Roderc] if not earlier," writes Alcock. "We must think of [Bede's] *civitas* . . . in an organizational sense, as an administrative and social center."[412]

HADRIAN'S WALL   Probable

Description:
Defensive wall with associated forts and "milecastles"

Dating Evidence:
Late fourth century *solidi* (Valentinian I to Maximus)
Two coins of Arcadius (c.395-408)
One coin of Honorius
Gold and glass earring (late fourth century)
Huntcliff Ware (late fourth century)
Crambeck Ware (fifth century)
"British" metalwork (fifth century)
"Anglo-Saxon" pottery (fifth century)
"Anglo-Saxon" metalwork and glass (sixth century)
"Anglo-Saxon" spearheads
"Anglo-Saxon" brooches (fifth/sixth century)
"Anglian" pin and brooch (eighth century)

Sources:
Bidwell, Paul T. *The Roman Fort of Vindolanda at Chesterholm, Northumberland*. London: Historic Buildings and Monuments Commission, 1985.
Bidwell, Paul and Stephen Speak. "South Shields." *Current Archaeology* 116 (1989): 283-87.
Birley, R. "Vindolanda." *Current Archaeology* 116 (1989): 275-79.
Breeze, David J. and Brian Dobson. *Hadrian's Wall*. 3rd edition. London: Penguin, 1987.
Crow, J.G. *Housesteads Roman Fort*. London: English Heritage, 1989.
Dark, K.R. "A Sub-Roman Re-Defense of Hadrian's Wall?" *Britannia* 23 (1992): 111-20.
Dore, J.N. *Corbridge Roman Site*. London: English Heritage, 1989.
Frere, S.S. *et al.* "Roman Britain in 1987." *Britannia* 19 (1988): 416-508.
Hadrian's Wall Ordnance Survey Map. Maybush, Southampton: Ordnance Survey, 1989.
Mann, J.C., ed. *The Northern Frontier in Britain from Hadrian to Honorius: Literary and Epigraphic Sources*. Newcastle: Museum of Antiquities, 1969.
Selkirk, Andrew and Tony Wilmott. "Birdoswald: Dark-Age Halls in a Roman Fort?" *Current Archaeology* 116 (1989): 288-91.
Welsby, Derek A. *The Roman Military Defense of the British Provinces in its Later Phases*. BAR British Series No. 101. Oxford: BAR Publishing, 1982.

The notion that the forts along Hadrian's Wall were abandoned following the troop withdrawals of Magnus Maximus and Constantine III was accepted for a long time. Now it is absolutely clear that the Wall was not abandoned, for excavation is revealing plentiful evidence of occupation continuing at the Wall forts after new coinage ceased to arrive in the early fifth century.[413] In fact, archaeologists have recently discovered new timber structures being built inside some of the forts which indicate occupation into the sixth century and beyond.

CASTLESTEADS (*Camboglanna*) is unique among the Wall forts in being built between the Vallum and the Wall. Radford identified a Class-I inscribed stone at Castlesteads which is thought to be of sixth-century date.[414]

BIRDOSWALD (*Banna*) fort was built to guard the Irthing bridge crossing. Recent excavations here have revealed the re-use of Roman military buildings as domestic structures in the fifth century, associated with the latest Romano-British pottery found in northern Britain.[415] Two Roman granaries were, in their final stages, reconstructed and used for human occupation. One of these new structures—termed "halls" by the excavators—was a modification of the south granary, while the other was built after the north granary had collapsed, partly overlying the granary, and partly overlying the adjacent Roman road.[416] Under the floor of the south granary was a fill of earth and rubbish containing Huntcliff and Crambeck Wares (late fourth to fifth centuries), and a hearth found at one end of the this "hall" contained a Roman gold and glass earring (later fourth century). Traces of fifth-century British metalwork were also uncovered, and on the other side of the fort an "Anglian" pin and brooch (eighth century) was found in the 1950s.[417]

CHESTERHOLM (*Vindolanda*) is the site of several forts, the first timber fort being part of the old Stanegate frontier system. An earthen bank piled against the fort wall suggests the possibility of post-Roman fortifications. Evidence for internal occupation in the sub-Roman period includes an "Anglo-Saxon" style annular brooch (sixth century?) and a fifth- or sixth-century penannular brooch, both found within the fort.[418] Outside the fort was found a Class-I inscribed tombstone (dated late fifth or early sixth century) which commemorates the death of one "Brigomaglos."[419] Thus, at Chesterholm we have a curious mixture of Romano-British and Germanic elements within the same community, suggesting the possible presence of Germanic merceneries.

HOUSESTEADS (*Vercovicium*) fort is the best preserved site on Hadrian's Wall. A seemingly prosperous *vicus*, with numerous shops and temples, grew up to the south and east of the fort. A defensive earthen bank was built after the fort's stone walls, and evidence of internal occupation includes sixth-century "Anglo-Saxon" pottery and metalwork.[420] It has also been suggested that some of the population of both Housesteads and Chesterholm relocated inside the Iron Age hillfort at Barcombe, which seems to preserve part of the name *Vercovicium*.[421]

CHESTERS (*Cilurnum*) was a bridgehead fort guarding the point where the Wall crosses the North Tyne river. Post-Roman occupation inside the fort is indicated by an "Anglo-Saxon" annular brooch of the sixth or seventh century.[422]

CORBRIDGE (*Corstopitum/Coriosopitum*) is a fort two miles south of the Wall which dates back to the first century. Like Housesteads, a large and prosperous *vicus* grew up around the stone-walled fortress. The main street of the town received its last resurfacing in the latter half of the fourth century, and a hoard of 48 gold coins found in Corbridge dates to this period.[423] Other coin finds (nine coins of Arcadius and Honorius) show that the town was occupied at least to the end of the fourth century.[424] Fifth- and sixth-century finds within the fort include "Anglo-Saxon" pottery and brooches.[425]

BENWELL (*Condercum*) fort was named by its Roman inhabitants "The Place with a Fine View." Sixth-century "Anglo-Saxon" glass and metalwork was found near the fort.[426]

SOUTH SHIELDS (*Arbeia*) fort is the easternmost settlement along the Wall, built to protect supplies entering the mouth of the River Tyne. Around 400, the southwest gate went out of use and a large ditch was dug in front of it.[427] Subsequent to this, the ditch was filled in and a new approach road was laid, and the gate—by this time in ruins—was replaced by a new gate passage contructed in timber. Associated finds include a gold *solidus* of Magnus Maximus, which has been dated to 388,[428] and an "Anglo-Saxon" spearhead.[429] Outside the fort was a small inhumation cemetery, possibly fifth- or sixth-century.[430]

Other miscellaneous finds from the Wall include an "Anglo-Saxon" spearhead from CARVORAN (*Magnis*) and a horde of late Roman coins (including one of Honorius) thrown as a votive offering into Coventina's Well at CARRAWBURGH (*Brocolitia*).[431]

If, as it appears, the Wall was not completely abandoned when coin payments stopped arriving after 410, what became of the soldiers stationed there? According to Breeze and Dobson, "we must accept that the soldiers of the Wall returned to the soil from which they had sprung"; i.e. back to the British communities into which they had been born or into which they had married.[432] Some undoubtedly remained as paid protectors of these northern *vici*, while others would have gravitated toward the new political and military powers of the north: Rheged, Strathclyde, and Manau Gododdin.[433]

Kenneth Dark has recently surveyed the fifth- and sixth-century evidence from the Wall and has developed an interesting scenario. The timber halls, inscribed tombstones, and post-Roman defenses are seen as secular high-status British re-use of the Wall forts, perhaps as a continuation or revival of the command of the *Dux Britanniarum*.[434] The presence of early Anglo-Saxon weapons within these Romano-British settlements is interpreted as a sign that the Britons were hiring Germanic merceneries, as indeed Gildas says they were doing. "We may have, then," writes Dark, "a pattern of probably secular high-status British reuse of a series of Wall-forts, and possibly the installation of Anglo-Saxon merceneries at them, and of the sub-Roman occupation of the nearby Roman-period towns of Corbridge and Carlisle."[435]

LINCOLN (*Lindum*)   Probable

Description:
Colonia

Dating Evidence:
Radiocarbon dating of graves (fifth century)
Imported pottery (Biv)

Sources:
Eagles, B.N. *The Anglo-Saxon Settlement of Humberside*. BAR No. 68. Oxford: BAR Publishing, 1979.
Gilmour, B. "The Anglo-Saxon Church at St. Paul-in-the-Bail, Lincoln." *Medieval Archaeology* 23 (1979): 214-18.
Jones, Michael J. "The Latter Days of Roman Lincoln." In *Pre-Viking Lindsey*, ed. A. Vince, pp. 14-28. Lincoln: City of Lincoln Archaeology Unit, 1993.
Jones, Michael J. et al. *The Archaeology of Lincoln, Vol. VII-1: The Defenses of the Upper Roman Enclosure*. Lincoln: Archaeological Trust, 1980.
Selkirk, Andrew. "Dark Earth and the End of Roman Lincoln." *Current Archaeology* 129 (1992): 364-67.
Stafford, Pauline. *The East Midlands in the Early Middle Ages*. Leicester: Leicester Univ. Press, 1985.
Steane, K. "St. Paul-in-the-Bail: A Dated Sequence." *Lincoln Archaeology* 3 (1991): 28-31.
Todd, Malcolm. *The Coritani*. Gloucester: Sutton, 1991.

The *Colonia Domitiana Lindensium*, or *Lindum*, succeeded an earlier legionary fortress at Lincoln. Little is known about the streets and buildings of the *colonia*, which lies beneath the medieval castle and cathedral in the heart of the modern city. Thus, most conclusions about sub-Roman Lincoln have been drawn according to what has not been found rather than what has.

Wacher points out that there are remarkably few zoomorphic buckles and fittings of the late Roman army in all of Lincolnshire, and only one in Lincoln itself.[436] There are no early Anglo-Saxon settlements attested in or near *Lindum* (the closest is some two miles north of the modern city limit), while a sixth-century king of Lindsey has an unmistakably British name—Caedbaed.[437] When an Anglian settlement finally does appear at Lincoln in the late seventh century, Bede tells us that the ruler in the area was a *praefectus Lindocolinae civitatis*, giving the British form (*Lindocolina*) of the city's name.[438]

Excavations at Lincoln have revealed some positive evidence for survival of occupation into the sub-Roman period. Street surfaces within the city were repaired in the fifth century, and there have been stray finds of imported Mediterranean pottery and a pin of "Celtic" design which could prolong occupation into the sixth century or later.[439] Evidence of a possible Christian community at Lincoln comes from the courtyard area at the forum. There, beneath the graveyard of a seventh-century Anglian church, lay other burials which have yielded radiocarbon dates centering in the fifth century.[440] It has been suggested that a timber church, destroyed by the construction of the Angilan stone church, was built on this site c.400 with a sub-Roman cemetery laying close to its walls.[441]

MOTE OF MARK   Definite

Description:
Hillfort with metalworking industry

Dating Evidence:
Imported pottery (D and E ware)
Imported "Germanic" glass (fifth/sixth century)
Interlace-decorated molds (sixth century?)
"British" penannular brooches and pins (sixth century)
Radiocarbon estimates (indeterminate)

Sources:
Alcock, Leslie. "Gwyr y Gogledd: An Archaeological Appraisal." *Archaeologia Cambrensis* 132 (1983): 1-18.
Graham-Campbell, James *et al*. "The Mote of Mark and Celtic Interlace." *Antiquity* 50 (1976): 48-53.
Laing, Lloyd. "The Mote of Mark and the Origins of Celtic Interlace." *Antiquity* 49 (1975): 98-108.
—. *Settlement Types in Post-Roman Scotland*. BAR No. 13. Oxford: BAR Publishing, 1975.
Longley, David. "The Date of the Mote of Mark." *Antiquity* 56 (1982): 132-34.

The Mote of Mark is set on a craggy hillock rising above a side estuary of the Solway Firth. Its summit is enclosed by a timber-reinforced stone wall, which was clearly destroyed by fire at some point in the site's history. The enclosed area is approximately 75m x 35m, but much of it is covered with rocky outcrops. Excavations in 1913, 1973, and 1979 uncovered an enormous amount of jewelry and metalworking debris, including what may be the first instance of Celtic interlace.[442]

There has been much debate concerning the nature and date of this fort. At first, excavators thought that they had uncovered an Iron Age hillfort reoccupied in the eighth century. The subsequent finds of imported Gaulish pottery and "Germanic" glass indicate occupation in the fifth and sixth centuries, while radiocarbon samples from the rampart show that it too was a post-Roman construction.[443] There is no evidence of Iron Age occupation at the Mote.

More accurate dating thus depends upon the stylistic evidence of the jewelry along with the imported pottery. Laing has argued that the brooches and pins as well as the interlace-decorated molds are purely "British" in style and are contemporary with the pottery, giving a sixth-century date to the industrial activity at the Mote.[444] His opponents argue that the interlace is zoomorphic and belongs to a later, seventh-century Anglian phase.[445] Alcock has pointed out that the fortification of hilltops was quite unknown in Anglo-Saxon Northumbria, and thus the ramparts at the Mote of Mark must pre-date Anglian settlement.[446] He suggests that the site was a British industrial foundation of the sixth century, whose jewelry industry was taken over by the Angles in the seventh.[447] Laing, on the other hand, dates the initial British occupation to the fifth century, with a defensive rampart built in the sixth, and believes that the site was abandoned when the Angles arrived in the seventh.[448]

There is also much debate on how to classify the site. The defensive rampart would suggest that the Mote of Mark is one of the many fortified hilltop settlements which appear throughout the "Celtic fringe" in the sub-Roman period. Alcock, who has excavated several of these, sees the Mote as "a princely *llys* [court] with an attendant jeweller."[449] But the profusion of jewelry-making debris suggests that the Mote could have been a purely industrial site, with its own defenses, which continued functioning as such after its ramparts were destroyed by fire and Angles controlled the territory.[450] "They took over the industrial activities of the Mote," writes Alcock, "and no doubt its British craftsmen as well, and exploited them vigorously for the production of elaborate jewelry in an early Anglo-Celtic style."[451]

RAVENGLASS (*Glannoventa*)   Possible

Description:
Roman fort and *vicus*

Dating Evidence:
Late fourth-century pottery
One *solidus* of Theodosius (379-395)

Sources:
Anonymous. "Note on Ravenglass." *Britannia* 8 (1977): 378.
Higham, Nicholas and Barri Jones. *The Carvetii*. Gloucester: Sutton, 1985.
Potter, T.W. *Romans in North-West England*. Kendal, Cumbria: T. Wilson, 1979.

The Roman fort of Ravenglass has yielded an unusually large quantity of late fourth-century pottery, "probably several hundred vessels."[452] Pottery and coinage bring the occupation at Ravenglass most likely to the early fifth century, whence it may have fitted into a "localized system of defense."[453] Ravenglass has also been suggested as a candidate for the hometown of St. Patrick, *Glannoventa* possibly being corrupted as *Banna Venta*.[454]

WHITHORN (*Candida Casa*)   Definite

Description:
Early Christian site

Dating Evidence:
Inscribed memorial stones (fifth and sixth centuries)
Imported Mediterranean *amphorae* (c.470-550)

Sources:
Hill, Peter. *Whithorn 2: Excavations 1984-7, Interim Report*. Whithorn: Whithorn Trust, 1988.
—. *Whithorn 3: Excavations 1988-90, Interim Report*. Whithorn: Whithorn Trust, 1990.
—. *Whithorn 4: Excavations 1990-1, Interim Report*. Whithorn: Whithorn Trust, 1992.
MacQueen, John. *St. Nynia*. Edinburgh: Polygon, 1990.
Oram, R.D. *A Journey Through Time 1: The Christian Heritage of Wigtownshire*. Whithorn: Whithorn Trust, 1987.
—. *A Journey Through Time 2: The Archaeology of Wigtownshire*. Whithorn: Whithorn Trust, 1987.

Bede tells us that the first Christian missionary in Scotland was a bishop named Ninian, a Briton who had studied in Rome. He founded a church in southern Scotland, at a place the English call *Hwit-aern*, and named it *Candida Casa* in honor of St. Martin of Tours. Bede, furthermore, describes this church as made of stone rather than wood, "in a manner to which the Britons were not accustomed."[455]

Although the historicity of St. Ninian's mission has been in question for some time, recently archaeology has thrown new light upon the very real early Christian community at Whithorn. Peter Hill's extensive excavations have uncovered both an early church and a later monastery which pre-date the Viking settlement at Whithorn. Phase 1/A (late fifth century) is dated by the presence of imported pottery and is characterized by small buildings. At one structure, isolated on the crown of a hill, diggers found the residue of lime which had been imported for white-washing—as close as archaeology will ever get to Ninian's "shining house (*candida casa*)."[456] Hill elaborates on these features:

> The buildings [of Phase 1] were consistently small and were probably rectilinear with bowed sides and straight end walls. The curving ditches may reflect overhanging eaves. No substantial timbers were used and the walls and roof were probably constructed as a single entity of woven wattle.[457]

Phase 1/B (late fifth to mid sixth century) extended to the last of the Mediterranean imports and saw the growth of the settlement, including a monastic (?) garden.[458] Phase 1/C (c.550-700) included buildings which were part of a secular settlement which grew up on the fringes of the ecclesiastical site; they yielded broken "wine glasses."[459]

Phase 1 ended with a possible disaster—a fire—and ceased contact with the outside world.[460] The period which followed, Phase 2 (late sixth century), saw the foundation of a cemetery of lintel graves closely linked with a circular shrine.[461] This has been identified as a monastic (?) oratory, and may have been associated with a small stone chapel.[462]

According to Hill, "The cumulative evidence of exotic technologies" uncovered at Whithorn—which includes lime-washing, mouldboard ploughs, and a mechanical mill—"suggests settlers with skills acquired within the Roman empire."[463] Charles Thomas, who has also excavated in the area, agrees that there must have been Romanized communities along the Galloway coast, perhaps with a sizeable enough Christian element in the late fourth century to warrant the provision of a bishop (from Carlisle?) such as Ninian.[464] Further evidence that such communities did exist is the impressive number of inscribed memorial stones from Galloway and Dumfrieshire. One, from Whithorn, was erected by a Christian family (it bore the formula *Te Dominum Laudamus*) to commemorate one *Latinus*.[465] Two stones from nearby Kirkmadrine (across Luce Bay) bear *Chi-Rho* crosses and have been dated c.500. One of these commemorates *Viventius* and *Mavorius* as *sancti et praecipui sacerdotes*, indisputable evidence of two priests bearing Latinized names in remote Galloway.[466]

YEAVERING (*Gefrin*)   Possible

Description:
Palisaded enclosure

Dating Evidence:
"Anglo-Saxon" pottery
Frankish buckle (sixth or seventh century)
Copy of a Merovingian gold *tirens* (c.630-50)

Sources:
Alcock, Leslie. "The North Britons, the Picts and the Scots." In *The End of Roman Britain*, ed. P.J. Casey, pp. 134-42. BAR British Series No. 71. Oxford: BAR Publishing, 1979.
—. "Gwyr y Gogledd: An Archaeoogical Appraisal." *Archaeologia Cambrensis* 132 (1983): 1-18.
—. *Bede, Eddius and the Forts of the North Britons*. Jarrow Lecture, 1988.
Hope-Taylor, Brian. *Yeavering: An Anglo-British Center of Early Northumbria*. London: HMSO, 1977.

Brian Hope-Taylor's excavations at Yeavering revealed a remarkable, though perhaps not unique, settlement type: a northern British fortress taken over by Angles which becomes an Anglian *villa regia*. The earliest structures at Yeavering—small timber and wattle buildings—are identified as "British" type, of fifth- or sixth-century date. Also thought to be British in origin is the double-palisaded Great Enclosure, which later became an elaborate structure associated with the Anglian Great Hall. Its initial phase consisted of two widely spaced parallel fences attached by two bulbous terminals, each enclosing a rectangular building which may have served as a look-out tower or guard post.[467] Both Hope-Taylor and Alcock believe that this enclosure was originally a place for public gatherings and part of a pre-Anglian royal center of the northern Britons, probably in the kingdom of the Gododdin.[468] "Yeavering's archaeological record clearly testifies to the meeting of two major cultural groups," writes the excavator, "each with diverse strains of influence already within it, at a time probably nearer 550 than 600; and to the vigorous hybrid culture which that produced."[469]

Other structures at Yeavering are more difficult to place, ethnically and chronologically. The enigmatic Building E was identified by the excavator as "unmistakably" a wooden theatre, focused on a stage (which may have carried a throne!) and a (carved?) ceremonial pole.[470] "Yeavering-style building," writes Hope-Taylor, "may well have been a response to the special political needs and pretensions of a ruling class ... [who] would be found not to have been without various enrichments and a certain crude pomp."[471] Datable objects from Yeavering include a silver-inlaid iron buckle of Frankish origin, which likely dates between c.570-80 and c.630-40, and a gold-washed copper alloy copy of a Merovingian gold *tirens*, minted c.630-50.[472]

YORK (*Eburacum*) Possible

Description:
Colonia

Sources:
Carver, M.O.H. et al. *The Archaeology of York Vol. IV, Part 1: Riverside Structures and a Well in Skeldergate and Buildings in Bishophill*. London: CBA, 1978.
Faull, Margaret L. "Settlement and Society in North-East England in the Fifth Century." In *Settlement and Society in the Roman North*, ed. P.R. Wilson, pp. 49-52. Bradford, West Yorkshire: Yorkshire Archaeological Society, 1984.
Ottaway, P. "Colonia Eburacensis: A Review of Recent Work." In *Archaeological Papers from York Presented to M.W. Barley*, ed. P.V. Addyman and V.E. Black, pp. 28-33. York: Archaeological Trust, 1984.
Ramm, H.G. "The End of Roman York." In *Soldier and Civilian in Roman Yorkshire*, ed. R.M. Butler, pp. 178-99. Leicester: Leicester Univ. Press, 1971.
Welsby, Derek A. *The Roman Military Defenses of the British Provinces in its Later Phases*. BAR British Series No. 101. Oxford: BAR Publishing, 1982.

There is no doubt that York enjoyed a special status among Romano-British cities in the third and fourth centuries. This former legionary fortress was used as headquarters for the campaigning emperors Septimius Severus and Constantius Chlorus, both of whom died in the city. York also saw the elevation of Constantine I, and was rewarded with impressive walls and fortifications.

Excavations in York have so far concentrated on the military and defenses, and we know little about its public and domestic buildings. The best evidence for fifth-century occupation comes from the headquarters building (*principia*) and the legionary bath-house.[473] The *principia*, in fact, remained intact and in use until it was destroyed by fire in the early seventh century or later.[474] A rise in the water level in the late fourth century caused severe flooding in York, resulting in the destruction of much of the wharves and harbor facilities.[475] York probably did not survive as a "center of population," writes Campbell, but it did survive as a "center of authority."[476] In 601, Pope Gregory the Great instructed Augustine to send a bishop to York who would become the metropolitan of "that city and province."[477] When the bishop Paulinus arrived in York in c.625, it was part of the Anglian kingdom of Edwin of Northumbria, who is said to "have brought under his sway all the territories inhabited by the Britons."[478]

Notes

[1] New settlements identifiable as "Germanic" (i.e. Anglian, Saxon, Jutish, etc.) or Irish are not included in the Gazetteer.

[2] See also the gazetteer of "Definite Sites" and "Possible Sites" in Edwards and Lane, eds., *Early Medieval Settlements in Wales*, 17; "Category A: Certainly Defended" and "Category B: Certainly Occupied" in Elizabeth A. Alcock, "Appendix: Defended Settlements," 58-59; those yielding imported pottery in idem, "Enclosed Places, AD 500-800," 40-46; and the Dumnonian sites in Elizabeth A. and Leslie Alcock, "Catalogue of Fortified Sites," 168-71.

[3] Bennett, "Canterbury," 128; Brooks, "The Case for Continuity," 103.

[4] Blockley, 206-7.

[5] Johns and Potter, 337-38. The dates of the coins range from 360-404, but two coins of Honorius and one of Maximus were clipped. If the Canterbury hoard compares to those studied by Burnett (see Part One above), the clipping perhaps took place during the reign of Constantine III (407-11), though it could have occurred later. Johns and Potter state "that the hoard was not deposited before the second decade of the fifth century." Grierson and Mays (18) accept this *terminus post quem*.

[6] For the influence that pre-existing communities of Christian Britons had on the conversion of the Anglo-Saxons and on the reestablishment of episcopal dioceses in Anglo-Saxon England, see Steven Bassett, "Church and Diocese in the West Midlands: the Transition from British to Anglo-Saxon Control," in *Pastoral Care Before the Parish*, ed. J. Blair and R. Sharpe (Leicester: Leicester Univ. Press, 1992), 13-40. Cf. Bassett, "Churches in Worcester Before and After the Conversion of the Anglo-Saxons," *Antiquaries Journal* 69 (1989): 230: "[The placement of English sees in Roman towns was] a clear acknowledgement of the extent to which Romano-British tribal capitals and other central places had remained politically (or often economically) important."

[7] Bennett, "Canterbury," 128.

[8] Esmonde Cleary, *The Ending*, 151: "Roman civic norms were no longer being adhered to at Canterbury."

[9] Ibid.

[10] Kent *et al.*, 371-73.

[11] Ibid., 372; Blackburn, "Three Silver Coins," 173-74.

[12] Drury, "Chelmsford," 168.

[13] Ibid.

[14] Ibid., 169.

[15] Ibid.; John S. Wacher, *The Towns of Roman Britain* (Berkeley, CA: Univ. of Cal. Press, 1974), 200; Rodwell and Rowley, 172. Domestic activity is indicated by rubbish pits, a collapsed oven, fragments of a bone comb, and a polychrome bead.

[16] Dunnett, *Trinovantes*, 142.

[17] Down, *Roman Chichester*, 101; Laing and Laing, *Celtic Britain*, 78.

[18] Down (*Roman Chichester*, 103) suggests a date of 408 for this coin. However, the coin has the reverse legend VICTORIA AUG, which is only found on the Arcadius AE 4 (*RIC* 187/63c) struck in 383. See Grierson and Mays, 102-3.

[19] Down, *Roman Chichester*, 103. The *solidus* is in mint condition and may never have circulated, and Down suggests that it was held as "bullion" by a trader waiting to pay for imported goods. Cf. Blackburn, "Three Silver Coins," 173-74.

[20] Welch, *Early Anglo-Saxon Sussex*, 14-15; and idem, "Late Romans," 322. Evidence includes coins ranging in date from AD 97-395, and crude hand-made pottery termed "Thundersbarrow ware." These wares appear to have replaced the mass-produced pottery which was no longer available by the beginning of the fifth century.

[21] Down, *Roman Chichester*, 101.

[22] Philip Crummy, *Colchester Report 3*, 18. Early (1853 and 1927-29) excavations at the Gate detected much charcoal, scorched stone, and grey soil indicating three successive fires. The middle fire layer sealed a damaged bronze coin with legible diademed head, a symbol which occurs from 307 onward.

[23] Clarke, *Roman Colchester*, 48. Twelve coins issued between 388 and 402 were recorded but not cataloged.

[24] See Dunnett, *Trinovantes*, 137; and P. Crummy, *Colchester Report 1*, 23.

[25] Such graves, usually identified as "early Saxon," have also been found within the town walls at Winchester, Portchester, and Dorchester-on-Thames. See P. Crummy, *Colchester Report 1*, 22.

[26] See P. Crummy, "A Roman Church."

[27] Ibid., 408.

[28] Milne, *From Roman Basilica*, 29.

[29] Milne, *The Port*, 33.

[30] Ibid.; Morris, *Londinium*, 329-30.

[31] Hall and Merrifield, 14.

[32] Ibid.; Painter, "Silver Ingot." The Arcadius issues were from Rome and Ravenna, the Honorius issue from Milan: see *RIC, Vol. X*, clxxv.

[33] Perring, 127; Merrifield, 226.

[34] Perring, 128; Hall and Merrifield, 14-16.

[35] Theodosian bronze coinage including, presumably, the Honorius AE 4 issued between 395 and 402. These were the last copper/bronze issues to reach Britain.

[36] There is one lone fifth-century example of a sunken-floored structure, built **within** the shell of a Roman building, at Pudding Lane: see Perring, 128.

[37] Palmer, 19. These inhumations were found immediately outside the walls of a Roman bath/house complex, which had been abandoned c.400.

[38] *The Anglo-Saxon Chronicle* (The Laud [Peterborough] Chronicle), *sub annum 456*: "In this year Hengest and Aesc fought against the Britons . . . and slew four companies; and the Britons then forsook Kent and fled to London in great terror."

[39] Perring, 129-30: "Cities remained symbols of authority for post-Roman communities, whose rulers maintained them to justify their own power."

[40] Martin Biddle, "Towns," in *The Archaeology of Anglo-Saxon England*, ed. D.M. Wilson (London: Methuen, 1976), 99-150 (106).

[41] Munby, 162; Cunliffe, *Portchester, Vol. II*, 301.

[42] See Munby, 162: "It is difficult to say whether a civilian population took over an abandoned fort, or whether a military militia together with their families formed a continuing military garrison. Certainly the fort was occupied up to the end of Roman Britain and [possibly] beyond."

[43] Cunliffe, *The Regni*, 132.

[44] Ibid.; Cunliffe, *Portchester, Vol. II*, 301.

[45] Blagg, "Richborough," 145; Welsby, 131; Grierson and Mays, 26. 60,000 Roman coins were recorded from the 1922-38 excavations, the majority of which were bronze.

46 Blagg, "Richborough," 145.

47 Ibid.

48 Stephen Johnson, *Later Roman Britain* (London: Paladin, 1986), 193.

49 This series is discussed in detail by Frere, *Verulamium*, 319; Laing and Laing, *Celtic Britain*, 74-75; Branigan, *Catuvellauni*, 191; and Esmonde Cleary, *The Ending*, 148-51. The coins (from all *insulae*) are discussed in Reece, "The Coins," in Frere, *Verulamium Excavations*, vol. 3, 3-17.

50 Branigan, *Catuvellauni*, 196. Cf. Esmonde Cleary, *The Ending*, 151: "The survival of Roman hydraulic techniques to such a late date is worthy of note." Frere (*Verulamium Excavations*, vol. 2, 226) estimates the dates based on the stratification of the associated structures discussed above. The only coins found beneath the pipe-trench were one of Constantius II (c.337-41), one of Constans (c.341-46), and one "small barbarous copy, *Fel. Temp. Reparatio* (horseman) type."

51 Branigan, *Town and Country*, 136.

52 Ibid.

53 Niblett, "Verulamium," 89; Selkirk and Niblett, 416-17.

54 Niblett, "Verulamium," 90-91.

55 This idea has been argued by R.E.M. Wheeler (1934), K.R. Davis (1982), and Sheppard Frere (1966). For discussion, see Laing and Laing, *Celtic Britain*, 74-75.

56 *Anglo-Saxon Chronicle* (Parker and Laud Chronicles), *sub annum* 571.

57 Biddle and Kjølbye-Biddle, 12.

58 Ibid., 13.

59 Ibid.

60 Our understanding of the transition from Roman paganism to Christianity in Verulamium is confused by the presence of large numbers of the latest (fourth-century) Roman coins in the city's pagan temples. See Selkirk and Niblett, 417. Niblett suggests three possible explanations for this evidence: 1) the temples were used as rubbish pits in the late Roman period, 2) the temples had converted to churches and Christians were dropping coins in them, or 3) pagan offerings continued to be made nearly 70 years after the temples were officially closed in the Empire.

61 Jenkins, "Ancient Camp."

62 Fox, "Some Evidence."

63 Silvester, "An Excavation," 89ff.

64 Ibid., 105-6.

65 Ibid., 103, 105.

66 Ibid., 114-16.

67 Barry C. Burnham and John Wacher, *The 'Small Towns' of Roman Britain* (London: Batsford, 1990), 174.

68 A.M. Burnett, "The Newton Mills, Bath, Treasure Trove," in *Coin Hoards from Roman Britain*, 193-98. A hoard of 255 silver *siliquae* was found in 1983 at Newton Mills Park near Bath. The coins range from one Trier *siliqua* of Constans (c.347-48) to 62 Trier *siliquae* of Magnus Maximus (383-88). Because the hoard lacks later issues of Maximus and his son Falvius Victor (elevated in 387), Burnett (194) suggests a deposition date of about 385, before the end of Maximus's minting of *siliquae* at Trier.

69 Burnham and Wacher, 175; Cunliffe, *Roman Bath*, 211.

70 The original account is in Cunliffe and Davenport, 74ff., where the excavators point out the time and care with which this sequence, in particular, was excavated. For discussion, see also Cunliffe, *The City*, 43-48; Esmonde Cleary, *The Ending*, 155-57; Burnham and Wacher, 175; and Laing and Laing, *Celtic Britain*, 76.

71 Cunliffe and Davenport, 11: "... excavation of the temple has demonstrated conclusively that substantial parts of the Roman structure remained standing for some considerable time, possibly into the seventh or eighth century, while surrounding ground-surfaces were sporadically repaired."

72 See Esmonde Cleary, *The Ending*, 157 ("The pottery experts seem to be over-compressing the sequence . . ."); Laing and Laing, *Celtic Britain*, 76 ("a very late [post-Roman] repaving of the temple precinct floor"); and Burnham and Wacher, 175 ("even on conservative estimates [the sequence] must have continued well into the fifth century if not beyond").

73 Cunliffe and Davenport, 11.

74 Ibid.; Cunliffe, *Roman Bath*, 209: "During period 5 we see the attempts of the late or sub-Roman population to keep the old building in use. . . ."

75 Cunliffe, *The City*, 48.

76 *Anglo-Saxon Chronicle* (F Lat), *sub annum* 577: "In this year Cuthwine and Ceawlin fought against the Britons and slew three kings, Coinmail, Condidan, and Farinmail, at the place which is called Dyrham; and they captured *tres civitates*, Gloucester, Cirencester, and Bath."

77 Bell, 80.

78 Ap Simon, 232-33. Three coins sealed in the original floor are of Constantine II and to c.330-37. The latest coins from the temple area are 18 struck between 364-75, and 3 struck between

383-95. One worn Theodosian coin was sealed by a fall of stones from the wall.

[79] Ibid., 82.

[80] Esmonde Cleary, *The Ending*, 184.

[81] Rahtz et al., *Cadbury Congresbury*, 2.

[82] Ibid.; Laing and Laing, *Celtic Britain*, 106; Alcock, *Economy*, 165: "Congresbury shows no signs of a hiatus, and the Roman pottery continued in use alongside the [Mediterranean] imports" of the fifth and sixth centuries.

[83] Rahtz et al., 231.

[84] Burrow, *Hillfort*, 157.

[85] Rahtz et al., 233. Dark (*Discovery*, 52) does not believe that the roundhouse was a pagan shrine.

[86] Alcock, *Economy*, 160; M.G. Fulford, "Byzantium and Britain," *Medieval Archaeology* 33 (1989): 1-5 (2). Cadbury-Congresbury is second only to Tintagel in quantity of imported wares.

[87] Rahtz et al., 2.

[88] Ibid., 249.

[89] Ibid., 250.

[90] Alcock, *Economy*, 183. Congar's *burg* becomes *Congresbury*.

[91] Rahtz et al., 250.

[92] P.J. Fowler in ibid., 249.

[93] Alcock, *Economy*, 212.

[94] Rahtz et al., 251.

[95] Ibid., 2, 251: "It cannot be claimed that it was declining fortunes in the west which ceased to attract distant traders and led to an end to the importation of pottery, glass and other goods; the causes are more likely to lie in the changing fortunes of the Mediterranean."

[96] Hanley, 55: "In Somerset there appears to have been a widespread transference of village settlements back into the local iron age hillforts."

[97] Laing and Laing, *Celtic Britain*, 72.

[98] Esmonde Cleary, *The Ending*, 184.

[99] Radford, "Castle Dore," 74-75; Radford and Swanton, 27.

[100] Most recently Quinnel and Harris, "Castle Dore."

[101] Rahtz, "Castle Dore—A Reappraisal," 53.

[102] Thomas, *A Provisional List*, 25.

[103] Williams in Quinnel and Harris, "Castle Dore," 129-30.

[104] Thomas, "Evidence"; idem, *Tintagel*, 96; Dark, *Discovery*, 79-80.

[105] Esmonde Cleary, *The Ending*, 125.

[106] Ann Woodward, *English Heritage Book of Shrines and Sacrifice* (London: Batsford/English Heritage, 1992), 88. At the Crown Buildings site, excavators found bits of clothing and a plait of red hair preserved by the plaster.

[107] Green, *Excavations, Vol. I*, 70-71; Esmonde Cleary, *The Ending*, 178-79.

[108] Green, *Excavations Vol. I*, 83; Farwell and Molleson, *Excavations, Vol. II*, 89.

[109] Philip Rahtz has interpreted this second phase settlement at Poundbury as a monastery: see Dark, *Discovery*, 46.

[110] Green, *Excavations, Vol. I*, 153.

[111] Bidwell, *Roman Exeter*, 86.

[112] Wacher, *Towns*, 334.

[113] Holbrook and Bidwell, 13.

[114] Bidwell, *Roman Exeter*, 86.

[115] Ibid.; Esmonde Cleary, *The Ending*, 152.

[116] Bidwell, *Roman Exeter*, 86.

[117] Ibid., 87. See also Philip Dixon, "'The cities are not populated as once they were,'" in *The City in Late Antiquity*, ed. John Rich (London: Routledge, 1992), 145-60 (147).

[118] Pearce, *Kingdom of Dumnonia*, 43: "The post-400 graveyard [at Exeter] testifies to the existence of a continuing community." Wacher, *Towns*, 335: "Certainly Britons continued to live peacefully in Exeter with Saxons until the early ninth century, when [the Britons] were expelled from the town."

[119] Wacher, *Towns*, 334-35.

[120] Ibid., 335; Johnson, *Later Roman Britain*, 201-2.

[121] Radford, "Glastonbury Abbey," 104-7. Radford was also led to this conclusion by the existence, in the twelfth century, of the shrines of saints Indracht and Patrick near the Abbey's old church: "St. Indracht and St. Patrick are Celtic saints, and it is difficult to believe that their cult was introduced at Glastonbury after the Saxon conquest of Somerset in the middle of the seventh century."

[122] Ellis, "Excavations."

[123] See Rahtz, "Pagan and Christian," 33; and Dark, *Discovery*, 46.

[124] Rahtz, "Glastonbury Tor," 115.

[125] The excavator believes the Roman objects to be of post-Roman use rather than representing a Roman settlement on the Tor: see Rahtz, *English Heritage Book of Glastonbury*, 54.

[126] Twenty miles away, at Pagans Hill, there is a late Roman temple comparable to those at Maiden Castle and Lydney. Yet this is hardly evidence for "a pagan revival," as suggested by Abrams and Carley, 7.

[127] Rahtz, "Glastonbury Tor," 121.

[128] E.g. Alcock, *Economy*, 190; and Dark, *Discovery*, 46.

[129] Rahtz, "Pagan and Christian," 32-33; idem, *English Heritage Book of Glastonbury*, 59.

[130] Dark (*Discovery*, 46), sees the Tor as "an island hermitage." Cf. Rahtz, *English Heritage Book of Glastonbury*, 60.

[131] William of Malmesbury, in the twelfth century, described Glastonbury Abbey as the oldest church in all of England. In William's day, the Glastonbury monks claimed that the Old Church was built by missionaries from Gaul in the second century. William also writes that the Irish tradition at Glastonbury was very strong. Several shrines in the Abbey contained the relics of Irish saints, including Patrick, who by tradition established a rule for the community about 460. The chapel at nearby Beckery had an early cult of St. Brigid, and claimed to possess this Irish saint's relics. The name *Bec Eriu*, "Little Ireland," makes the Irish connection explicit. Plausibly, Irish monastics could have frequented Glastonbury in the sixth century before the arrival of the West Saxons.

[132] These are recorded in Burrow, *Hillforts*, 268-77. The coins, however, are not cataloged.

[133] Ibid., 268. See also R.H. Leech, "Romano-British Rural Settlement in South Somerset and North Dorset" (Ph.D. Thesis, Univ. of Bristol, 1977), 119-21.

[134] Pollard, "Neolithic and Dark Age Settlements," 42.

[135] Ibid., 35.

[136] Ibid., 57. See also Dark, *Discovery*, 87.

[137] H. Miles, "Excavations," 89.

[138] Thomas, "Lundy," 139; idem, *A Provisional List*, 25.

[139] Thomas, "Lundy," 140-42.

[140] Ibid., 139.

[141] Wheeler, 334-35; Sharples, *Maiden Castle*, 130. Four gold *solidi* (three issues of Arcadius—one from Milan, two from Ravenna—and one issue of Honorius, from Milan) and a finger ring were found immediately outside the temple entrance, while a hoard of 70 coins (mostly Constantinian) were found in a pot on the surface of the fourth-century road south of the temple. Inside the temple, another hoard of coins (running to 367) was found sealed under the plain mosaic floor.

[142] Dark, *Discovery*, 51 n.199.

[143] Wheeler, 78.

[144] Sharples, *Maiden Castle*, 130.

[145] See Kent, *RIC, Vol. X*, cii.

[146] Wedlake, *The Excavation*, 82.

[147] Ibid., 86-87.

[148] Ibid., 109-10.

[149] Ibid., 117: "At the end of the fourth century there are enough coins of the House of Theodosius and, more surprisingly, copies of such coins to be reasonably sure that some substantial occupation continued up to, and beyond, the year 400." Wedlake (ibid., 109) is even more optimistic: "There is no apparent reason why this occupation should not have continued well beyond the date of the latest currency (AD 402) into the fifth and sixth centuries." See also Dark, *Discovery*, 50.

[150] See Pearce, *Dumnonia*, 66-67.

[151] Thomas, "Christians," 22.

[152] Ibid. Thomas also records an enigmatic "architectural fragment . . . of the fifth century."

[153] Ibid.

[154] Thomas, *Exploration*, 173.

[155] Ibid., 187; Susan M. Pearce, *The Archaeology of South West Britain* (London: Collins, 1981), 188.

[156] See Dark, *Discovery*, 80.

[157] Leach, 19.

[158] Ibid, 24.

[159] Ibid. Leach points out that this "is one of the most positive identifications ever made in Roman Britain of a Christian burial," and suggests that the amulet may have belonged to a priest.

[160] Ibid., 27.

[161] Alcock, *Economy*, 172-73.

162 Burrow, *Hillfort*, 157, based on the *Burghal Hidage* evidence of four men to every 5 1/2 yards of rampart.

163 Alcock, *Economy*, 186.

164 Ibid., 190.

165 Ibid., 182.

166 See discussion under Doon Hill and Yeavering below.

167 Alcock, *Economy*, 206-7.

168 See discussion under Wroxeter below.

169 Alcock, *Economy*, 207.

170 Ibid., 200-201.

171 Ibid., 182.

172 Ibid., 193, 196. Nailed timber ramparts—*murrus gallicus*—are most common in Iron Age western Europe, and were also used in the Pictish forts of Burghead and Dundurn.

173 Ibid., 182-83.

174 Ibid., 197.

175 Charles Thomas, *Celtic Britain* (London: Thames and Hudson, 1986), 73.

176 See Dark, review of *Tintagel*, 103-4.

177 Thomas, *Celtic Britain*, 71; Padel in Thomas, *A Provisional List*, 29.

178 Thomas, *Celtic Britain*, 75; A.L.F. Rivet and Colin Smith, *The Place-Names of Roman Britain* (Princeton: Univ. Press, 1979), 350.

179 Thomas, *Tintagel*, 13 and 84. Ten bronze coins, ranging from Tetricus I to Constantine II, were found in a drawstring leather purse. The pottery, dating to the fourth century, consisted of sherds of Oxford Red Colour-Coated ware as well as sherds from locally made jars and bowls.

180 Thomas, *Celtic Britain*, 75-76.

181 Malcolm Todd, *The South West to AD 1000* (London: Longman, 1987), 163; Thomas, *Tintagel*, 71. The total from Tintagel is greater than the total of all the sherds of "Tintagel ware" found at all sites in Britain and Ireland combined.

182 Thomas, *Tintagel*, 94-95. Cornwall was a major supply of tin for the Roman Empire. That it remained a sought-after commodity in the post-Roman world is affirmed by the account of the Byzantine ship returning from Britain loaded with tin in the sixth-century *Life of St. John the Almsgiver*. See Penhallurick, *Tin in Antiquity*, 245.

183 Dark, *Discovery*, 80-86.

184 Thomas, ed., *Tintagel Papers*, 46, 54.

185 Ibid., 19.

186 Morris *et al.*, 848.

187 Thomas, *Tintagel*.

188 Ibid., 85-86.

189 Ibid., 87. Cf. Dark, *Civitas*, 91ff.

190 See Thomas, *Tintagel*, 88; and Thomas Charles-Edwards, "Early Medieval Kingships in the British Isles," in *Origin of Anglo-Saxon Kingdoms*, ed. S. Bassett (Leicester: Leicester Univ. Press, 1989), 28ff.

191 Nowakowski and Thomas, 2; Thomas, *Tintagel*, 103. Pottery finds include sherds of Bi, Bii, Biv, and Bv *amphorae*.

192 Thomas, *Tintagel*, 103. If one adds a century to this date, to allow for the tree to mature, this gives a date of c.503 for the fire.

193 Ibid. The "arc crosses" carved in the Tintagel tombstones may also have been a continental borrowing.

194 Ibid., 105.

195 Nowakowski and Thomas, 2.

196 Pearce, *Dumnonia*, 49; Thomas, "A Provisional List," passim; Dark, *Discovery*, 86.

197 Pearce, *Dumnonia*, 49.

198 Thomas, *Tintagel*, 96. A crude stone furnace containing a block of smelted tin was found at another Cornish fortification, Chun Castle, which has also produced imported pottery.

199 Richard Morris, *The Church in British Archaeology*, CBA Report No. 47 (London: CBA, 1983), 26-28.

200 Ellison, *Excavations at West Hill*, 33-35.

201 Woodward and Leach, 318ff.

202 Ibid., 322.

203 Ibid., 321.

204 Ibid., 324ff.

205 Ibid., 189.

206 Ibid., 327.

207 Ibid., passim; Ellison, "Natives, Romans and Christians," passim.

[208] Clarke, *The Roman Cemetery at Lankhills*, 5, 105-7, 238. The graves contained one coin of Valentinian I (364-75), one bronze coin from the House of Theodosius (c.388-402), and 2 or 3 sherds of coarse pottery dated to the end of the fourth century.

[209] J.L. MacDonald, "Features 24, 25, and 26," in Clarke, *Roman Cemetery*, 107.

[210] Biddle, "Study of Winchester," 111-13.

[211] Wacher, *Towns of Roman Britain*, 288.

[212] Esmonde Cleary, *The Ending*, 132.

[213] Richard White, "Excavations at Aberffraw," 341.

[214] Edwards, "Aberffraw," 20-21. See also Laing and Laing, *Celtic Britain*, 108; Wendy Davies, *Wales in the Early Middle Ages* (Leicester: Leicester Univ. Press, 1982), 24.

[215] *ECMW* No. 27. Found at nearby Llangeinwen (five miles from Aberffraw), the side plates of the lead coffin bear the inscriptions CAMVLORIS H(ic?) O(ssa?) I(acent?), "Here lie the bones of Camulorix," and CAMVLORIS, "Camulorix." Nash-Williams states that such coffins are common among Christian inhumations in Britain and Gaul from the fourth century onwards, and dates this specimen to the fifth century. "Camulorix" seems to have been a popular name in sub-Roman Wales: cf. *ECMW* Nos. 349 and 403.

[216] Musson *et al.*, 65, 159.

[217] Ibid., 194; Dark, *Discovery*, 79.

[218] Gildas (*De Excidio*, 10.2) says that the British martyrs Aaron and Julius were "citizens of Caerleon (*Legionum urbis cives*)."

[219] Evans and Metcalf, 75: "The buildings have a *terminus post quem* of c.AD 354, but a far later date is almost certain."

[220] Ibid., 56.

[221] Ibid., 75; Lane, "Caerleon," 34.

[222] Evans and Metcalf, 75.

[223] W. Davies, *Wales*, 14.

[224] Esmonde Cleary, *The Ending*, 54; Derek A. Welsby, *The Roman Military Defense of the British Provinces in its Later Phases*, BAR British Series No. 101 (Oxford: BAR Publishing, 1982), 128. According to Boon ("Theodosian Coins," 429 n.4), the clipped *siliqua* found at Caernarvon most likely belongs to Theodosius. Cf. Davies, "Segontium," 115: "The practice of clipping *siliquae*, although confined to Britain, is more likely to be attributed to the decade 410-20 than in a post 430 era (pers. comm. Dr. J.P.C. Kent)."

[225] Laing, "Segontium," 57.

[226] Ibid., 57-59; W. Davies, *Wales*, 24, 82.

[227] Wacher, *Towns*, 388.

[228] Ibid., 189; Esmonde Cleary, *The Ending*, 145-46. Though there is evidence of gate-blocking in other towns, such as Colchester and Lincoln, it is not clear from the evidence whether this is in response to an external threat or the internal breakdown of security.

[229] Reece, "Numerical Aspects," 92; Knight and Lane, "Caerwent," 37. The Caerwent bronze hoards end with issues of Honorius: see Kent, *RIC, Vol. X*, cxxxiii.

[230] Wacher, *Towns*, 389.

[231] Ibid.

[232] Ibid.; Laing and Laing, *Celtic Britain*, 108; W. Davies, *Wales*, 24-25, 57.

[233] Laing and Laing, *Celtic Britain*, 108.

[234] Davies, "Roman Settlements," 154; Heather James, "Early Medieval Cemeteries in Wales," in *The Early Church in Wales*, ed. N. Edwards and A. Lane, Oxbow Monograph No. 16 (Oxford: Oxbow, 1992), 90-103 (96 and 103).

[235] Knight and Lane, "Caerwent," 37. Needless to say, this would have far-reaching implications for the traditional identification of Roman and sub-Roman sites in Britain.

[236] Evans, "Caldey Island," 43; Leach, "Ancient Graves," 174-75.

[237] Campbell, "New Finds," 61.

[238] Ibid., 59-60.

[239] Ibid., 61.

[240] James, "Early Medieval," 98; Dark, *Discovery*, 79.

[241] Campbell, "Coygan Camp," 45.

[242] Ibid., 45-46. The "counterfeiter's coin hoard" suggests the presence of a forger's workshop in the later third century. See also Wainwright, 70-71, 157-58; and Laing and Laing, *Celtic Britain*, 114.

[243] Campbell, "Coygan Camp," 45-46.

[244] Ibid., 46.

[245] Lane, "Deganwy Castle," 51-52.

[246] Ibid. 51; Laing and Laing, *Celtic Britain*, 114.

[247] Lane, "Degannwy Castle," 51, 124; Thomas, *A Provisional List*, 11, 18.

[248] See J.L. Davies's dating schemes in Lane, "Degannwy Castle," 52.

[249] Alcock (*Economy*) maintains the association, while Dumville ("Gildas and Maelgwn") believes that the evidence—from the *Annales Cambriae*—is no earlier than the tenth century.

[250] See, for example, John Morris, ed. and trans., *Nennius: British History and the Welsh Annals* (London and Chichester: Phillimore, 1980), 47; and Lane, "Degannwy Castle," 52.

[251] E. Campbell and J.L. Davies in Campbell, "Dinas Emrys," 56; Laing and Laing, "Scottish and Irish Metalwork," 213.

[252] Campbell, "Dinas Emrys," 56; Laing and Laing, *Celtic Britain*, 57-58.

[253] Campbell, "Dinas Emrys," 57.

[254] Alcock, *Economy*, 7.

[255] Ibid., 20-22.

[256] Ibid., 23 n.4.

[257] Laing and Laing, *Celtic Britain*, 55-57.

[258] Dr. I.W. Cornwall analyzed 1,677 bones in the 1950s, while Roberta Gilchrist anlayzed another 5,576 bones in 1987. See Alcock, *Economy*, 67-82.

[259] Gilchrist, 59.

[260] Gilchrist (61) questions Alcock's assumption that Dinas Powys was engaged in long-distance trade, preferring to see the princely stronghold engaged in "local exchange of animals primarily for their by-products."

[261] Esmonde Cleary, *The Ending*, 179.

[262] Gardner and Savory, 95-96; Dark, *Discovery*, 52.

[263] George C. Boon, "The Coins," in Gardner and Savory, 114-30 (126).

[264] Gardner and Savory, 95-96.

[265] Ibid., 99 and 205.

[266] Ibid., 99, 162, 188-89; Dark, *Discovery*, 76.

[267] Dating by E. Campbell and J.L. Davies in Lane, "Gateholm," 74.

[268] Ibid., 74.

[269] Davies in Ibid.

[270] Ibid., 74-75: "Consequently, it would seem likely that some of the settlement, if not all of it, is of early medieval date." Cf. Lethbridge and David, 374; Davies *et al.*, 104, 106.

[271] Lane, "Glan-y-Mor," 75.

[272] Ibid., 77.

[273] Ibid., 77-8; Evans *et al.*, 94, 103.

[274] Lane, "Glan-y-Mor," 77; Evans *et al.*, 63-68, 90.

[275] Lane, "Glan-y-Mor," 77; Evans *et al.*, 122; Dowdell, 344.

[276] Lane, "Glan-y-Mor," 77; Evans *et al.*, 108. "In short," writes Lane (78), "there is good reason to think that there was early medieval activity in the ruins of a Roman building at Glan-y-mor and possibly traces of a small building or buildings."

[277] Kelly, "Recent Research," 104.

[278] Ibid.; Kelly, "Graenog," 79.

[279] Campbell, "Longbury Bank," 88.

[280] Ibid., 88 and Appendix 1. Campbell describes one of these glass vessels as "from a cone-beaker with opaque white marvered trails identical to a vessel from Dinas Powys." See also Campbell and Lane, "Excavations at Longbury Bank," 15 and 21.

[281] Campbell and Lane, "Excavations at Longbury Bank," 15 and 21.

[282] Ibid.; Campbell, "Longbury Bank," 89.

[283] Alcock in Campbell, "Longbury Bank," 89.

[284] Ibid., 88; Green, "Excavations at Little Hoyle."

[285] Campbell, "Longbury Bank," 89.

[286] Campbell and Lane, "Excavations at Longbury Bank," 62. The authors (15) interpret Longbury as an "undefended high status secular site."

[287] Dark, *Discovery*, 98; Boon, "Theodosian Coins from North and South Wales," 434-35. The hoard was discovered at Holyhead Mountain Tower. The clipped *siliqua* bears the reverse legend VIRTVS ROMANORVM, which would place it in the date range 392-408.

[288] Smith, "Excavations . . . Part IV," 27ff.

[289] Ibid., 21, 29, and 34. Smith (25) states that these determinations "together form one of the tightest groups of radiocarbon dates the author has ever seen." See also Edwards, "Ty Mawr," 119-20; and Kelly, "Recent Research," 104.

[290] Kelly, "Recent Research," 104.

[291] Ibid., 120; Smith, "Excavations . . . Part II," 38.

292 Smith, "Excavations . . . Part IV," 36.

293 See Burnham and Wacher, 287-89.

294 See Dark, *Discovery*, 94.

295 Esmonde Cleary, *The Ending*, 57; Laing and Laing, *West Cheshire*, 42; McPeake, "The End," 43.

296 Strickland, "Chester," 6.

297 Ibid.

298 McPeake, "The End," 41.

299 Ibid., 43; Thomas, "A Provisional List", 25; Higham, *The Origins*, 65.

300 Higham, *The Origins*, 66.

301 Laing and Laing, *West Cheshire*, 42.

302 Higham, *The Origins*, 66.

303 Ward, 26.

304 Bede, *EH*, 2.2.

305 Ibid. This is corroborated by the *Annales Cambriae*, 613. The Laings see Bede's use of *civitas* as implying a thriving settlement. Cf. Higham, *The Origins*, 85.

306 Nennius, *Historia Brittonum*, 56. See also Rivet and Smith, 337.

307 Laing and Laing, *West Cheshire*, 27.

308 For a discussion of the significant topographical and literary evidence for the survival of Chester's Roman structures well into the medieval period, see Strickland, "The Roman Heritage of Chester."

309 Wacher, "Late Roman Developments," 15; Reece and Catling, 9.

310 Wacher, "Late Roman Developments," 15. Within the mortar of the masonry there was embedded a piece of color-coated pottery of the late fourth century.

311 Ibid., 16. The Laings (*Celtic Britain*, 76) point out that one of these bodies was found associated with medieval pottery.

312 See Wacher, *Towns*, 311; and Thomas, *Christianity*, 133.

313 Wacher, *Towns*, 311.

314 McWhirr et al., *Cirencester Excavations II*, 27; McWhirr, "Cirencester," 48. McWhirr believes that one of these cemeteries may have been in use well into the fifth or even the sixth century.

315 Wacher, "Late Roman," 17 n.11. Wacher cites "a personal communication with Dr. Richard Reece," but does not describe the coins.

316 Ibid.

317 McWhirr et al., *Cirencester Excavations II*, 27.

318 Reece and Catling, 9: "The church no doubt continued, a titular chief or king continued, but few buildings needed to be kept up for human occupation."

319 See Burnham and Wacher, 211-17.

320 See Dark, *Discovery*, 98 and n.308.

321 Hurst, "Major Saxon Discoveries," 254.

322 Heighway, *Anglo-Saxon Gloucestershire*, 3-5, 12; Dark, *Civitas*, 50.

323 Heighway, *Anglo-Saxon Gloucestershire*, 12.

324 Hurst, *Gloucester*, 123-24.

325 Hurst, "Excavations 1968-71," 58; Heighway et al., 159.

326 Heighway et al., 165.

327 Ibid., 163.

328 Laing and Laing, *Celtic Britain*, 76.

329 Ibid.; Hurst, "Excavations, 1971-3," 23. *Fel. Temp. Reparatio* coins were introduced in 348. Imitations, which occur predominantly in Britain, belong to the third quarter of the fourth century. See Grierson and Mays, 71; and Brickstock, 112-17.

330 Myfannwy Lloyd Jones, *Society and Settlement in Wales and the Marches 500 BC-AD 1100*, 2 vols., BAR British Series No. 121 (Oxford: BAR Publishing, 1984), 66.

331 The Romano-British pottery at Gloucester was not locally made—the shell-tempered ware came from the Midlands, the Oxfordshire ware from the Upper Thames Valley—which supports the view that Gloucester's forum remained an active marketplace in the sub-Roman period. See Heighway et al., 171.

332 Hurst, "Kingsholm," 272.

333 Bryant, "Excavations"; Heighway, *Anglo-Saxon Gloucestershire*, 10-11; R. Morris, *The Church in British Archaeology*, 26; idem, *Churches in the Landscape* (London: Dent, 1989), 35.

334 See Steven Bassett, "Churches in Worcester Before and After the Conversion of the Anglo-Saxons," *Antiquaries Journal* 69 (1989): 225-56 (243).

335 Zeepvat et al., 10.

336 Marney, 54.

337 Fulford, "Silchester," 328.

338 Boon, *Silchester*, 72.

339 Ibid.; Fulford, *Silchester Amphitheatre*.

340 Boon, *Silchester*, 73; Fulford, *Silchester Defences*, 237.

341 Boon, "The Latest Objects from Silchester," surveys most of this evidence.

342 Richard Morris (*The Church in British Archaeology*, 12) briefly summarizes the evidence.

343 Boon, *Silchester*, 72-73, 181-83. Though the basilical plan is also similar to some mystery-cult temples in Rome, the Silchester structure is different in that it contains a transept in front of the apse. Boon thus concludes (175): "This is the one particular element of the design which enables us to identify the building beyond doubt as a church."

344 Ibid., 173, 177-78; Boon, *The Roman Town*, 4. Richard Morris (*The Church in British Archaeology*, 12) suggests a date of c.360 or later.

345 Boon, *Silchester*, 77-78. It is perhaps significant that this inscription is not accompanied by Latin text, as are most Christian Ogom inscriptions. For the debate over the authenticity of this inscription, see M. Fulford and B. Sellwood, "The Silchester Ogham: A Reconsideration," *Antiquity* 54 (1980): 95-99; G.C. Boon, "The Silchester Ogham," *Antiquity* 54 (1980): 122-3; and Dark, *Civitas*, 150.

346 Boon, *Silchester*, 77-78; idem, *The Roman Town*, 8.

347 Boon, *Silchester*, 77; Laing and Laing, *Celtic Britain*, 75.

348 See Boon, *Silchester*, 78-80; Laing and Laing, *Celtic Britain*, 75; Wacher, *Towns*, 276 and 419; Esmonde Cleary, *The Ending*, 198; and Dark, *Civitas*, 101, 150-51. However, as Dark has pointed out, the Silchester dykes have not yet been securely dated.

349 Boon, *The Roman Town*, 8.

350 Webster, "A Roman System of Fortified Posts." See also Burnham and Walker, 276.

351 Webster, *Wall*, 8; Burnham and Wacher, 278.

352 *Historia Brittonum*, 66a.

353 Webster, *Wall*, 9. The Laings (*Celtic Britain*, 79), stating that Wall is the only (Roman?) town in the list that was not a cantonial capital, assume Nennius must have had special knowledge to prompt him to include it.

354 Webster, *Wall*, 9-10: "Here may be preserved in poetic form the memory of a clash between the Celtic pagan west and the remnants of the Romano-British Christian community in that twilight period in the fifth and sixth centuries before the advent of the Saxon settlers."

355 See Basset, "Church and Diocese," 34-35; and Jenny Rowland, *Early Welsh Saga Poetry: A Study and Edition of the Englynion* (Cambridge: Boydell and Brewer, 1990). Basset shows that there was a British see (and possibly a monastery) at sub-Roman Wall which was succeeded by St. Michael's church in the adjacent settlement of Lichfield. This could explain Eddius Stephanus's statement (*Life of Wilfrid*, ch. 15) that Lichfield was "a suitable place" to establish the see of the Mercians in 669. The see was given to the Irish-schooled Chad, who was consecrated (first) by schismatic **British** bishops.

356 Bassett, "Churches in Worcester," 243.

357 Barker et al., "Two Burials."

358 Bassett, "Churches in Worcester," 238-40; idem, "Church and Diocese in the West Midlands," 24ff.

359 Wacher, *Towns*, 373. Wacher points out that finds of lead-weighted javelins (*martiobarbuli*) indicate that "the regular army were passing through Wroxeter in the very late fourth or early fifth century."

360 Ibid..; White, "Excavations," 5.

361 Laing and Laing, *Celtic Britain*, 79.

362 White, "Excavations," 6.

363 Ibid. White suggests 420-50, though he takes for granted the collapse of Britain's money economy at this time.

364 Ibid.

365 Barker in Michael Wood, *In Search of the Dark Ages* (New York: Facts on File, 1987), 47.

366 Ibid.

367 White, "Excavations," 7. Cf. Esmonde Cleary, *The Ending*, 153: "The main phase of timber buildings is interpreted by the excavator as the residence and compound of a fifth-century notable."

368 Webster, *The Cornovii*, 117. This model, however, does not explain the relationship between the "villa" and the rest of the city, which seems to have shared in the renewed prosperity. Mike Corbishley (*Town Life in Roman Britain*, 47) notes the significance of the rebuilding of both public and private buildings in fifth-century Wroxeter.

369 Philip Dixon, "'The cities are not populated as once they were,'" in *The City in Late Antiquity*, ed. John Rich (London: Routledge, 1992), 145-60 (147).

[370] White, "Excavations," 7.

[371] Esmonde Cleary, *The Ending*, 152.

[372] White ("Excavations," 7) states that "... there is no evidence for a sack of the town by Anglo-Saxons, who moved into this area in the later 6th or early 7th century." Crickmore (*Romano-British*, 96) believes that the organized construction and abandonment at Wroxeter "suggest . . . some form of controlling authority."

[373] Thomas, *A Provisional List*, 16.

[374] Webster and Barker, 28. The full inscription, in Latin, reads CUNORIX MAQUS MAQUI COLONI, "Hound King, son of the Son of the Holly."

[375] Webster, *The Cornovii*, 114; Wacher, *Towns*, 374. See, however, Gelling, *The West Midlands*, 26-27: "I find it easier to think of Cunorix as a guest, a high-ranking visitor to a British court, whose hosts had sufficient courtesy and just sufficient literacy to give him a memorial in the style appropriate to his nationality. This stone seems to me a strong piece of evidence for the maintenance of a high-status sub-Roman lifestyle at Wroxeter far into the fifth century, probably in peaceful conditions."

[376] Burnham and Wacher, 239-40; Laing and Laing, *Celtic Britain*, 79.

[377] Wilson, "An Early Christian Cemetery;" Laing and Laing, *Celtic Britain*, 79.

[378] Burnham and Wacher, 240. The excavator's claim that these cremations date to "the period prior to AD 450" must, however, be taken with some suspicion.

[379] Thomas, "An Early Christian Cemetery," 127. See also R. Morris, *The Church in British Archaeology*, 51.

[380] Thomas, "An Early Christian Cemetery," 158-62.

[381] Ibid., 169, 174.

[382] Ferris and Jones; Esmonde Cleary, *The Ending*, 143.

[383] Welsby (131) postulates sub-Roman activity here.

[384] Dark, "A Sub-Roman Re-Defense," 112, 119-20.

[385] Crone, "Buiston."

[386] Ibid., 112-13.

[387] McCarthy, *A Roman, Anglian and Medieval Site at Blackfriars Street*, 45, 103, 369-72. These reconstructions are associated with 38 coins dating after 364 and ending with a coin of Arcadius.

[388] Burnham and Wacher, 58.

[389] Keevill *et al.*, 254. Two coins dating 341-46 and 364-75 were hidden between the floor slabs of the townhouse.

[390] A *solidus* of Valentinian II was found in the mud infill of the partly water-logged cellar of the townhouse. The *solidus* (*RIC* 9.90a) bears the obverse legend D N VALENTINIANVS P F AVG, and was minted between 388 and 392. See Keevil *et al.*, 254.

[391] Keevill *et al.*, 254: "The *solidus* suggests that the hypocaust fell from use at the end of the fourth or early fifth century. The room continued in use for a layer of *opus signium* 0.1m thick sealed the slab floor with a further two floor levels above. There are, therefore, strong grounds for believing that this building continued well into the fifth century." Cf. McCarthy *et al.*, 300: "This high-status building clearly continued in use for some considerable time into the fifth century."

[392] Higham and Jones, 133; Higham, *The Northern Counties*, 263.

[393] Thomas, *Christianity in Roman Britain*, ch. 13. This would appear even more likely if Carlisle was the capital of the late-formed province of *Valentia*. See also Burnham and Wacher, 52, 58.

[394] *Vita Sancti Cuthberti*, 4, written by an anonymous monk of Lindisfarne c.700. Cf. Burnham and Wacher, 51.

[395] Burnham and Wacher, 58.

[396] Burnham and Wacher, 116-17.

[397] Ibid.; Hartley and Fitts, 115.

[398] Burnham and Wacher, 117.

[399] Nick Higham, *The Northern Counties to AD 1000* (London: Longman, 1986), 263, 273.

[400] Alcock, "Gwyr y Gogledd," 15-17; idem, *Economy*, 250-54.

[401] Alcock, "Gwyr y Gogledd," 9; idem, *Economy*, 244.

[402] Reynolds, "Dark Age Timber Halls."

[403] Alcock, *Economy*, 244.

[404] Hope-Taylor, "Balbridie," 19.

[405] See Alcock, *Economy*, 244f.

[406] Alcock ("The Activities of Potentates," 28) cites evidence that the hall (which?) at Doon Hill was destroyed by fire.

[407] See Alcock, *Economy*, 162; and idem, "The Activities of Potentates," 31.

[408] Alcock, *Economy*, 235.

[409] Ibid., 235-36.

[410] Ibid., 235; Alcock, "The Activities of Potentates," 28.

[411] Alcock, *Economy*, fig. 16.3; Thomas, *A Provisional List*, 9-11, 20.

[412] Alcock, *Economy*, 236.

[413] Breeze and Dobson, 232: "It is certainly clear that the Wall was not abandoned as a result of these troop withdrawals."

[414] *RIB* No. 2331. See also Dark, "A Sub-Roman Re-Defense," 112 and n.10.

[415] Selkirk and Wilmott, 288-91; Dark, "A Sub-Roman Re-Defense," 112, 119-20; Laing and Laing, *Celtic Britain*, 119.

[416] Selkirk and Wilmott, 290.

[417] Ibid., 291.

[418] Frere *et al.*, 436-37; Dark, "A Sub-Roman Re-Defense," 111-12, 119-20.

[419] *CIIC*, vol. 1 (498). See Breeze and Dobson, 233; A.R. Burn, *The Romans in Britain: An Anthology of Inscriptions* (Columbia, SC: Univ. of S. Carolina Press, 1969), 177.

[420] Crow, 49; Dark, "A Sub-Roman Re-Defense," 119-20.

[421] Crow, 49-50.

[422] Dark, "A Sub-Roman Re-Defense," 112, 119.

[423] See Keevill *et al.*, "A Solidus of Valentinian II," 255. This hoard contained 4 coins of Valentinian I, 2 of Valens, 16 of Gratian, 8 of Valentinian II, 5 of Theodosius I, and 13 of Magnus Maximus.

[424] Dore, 27; Breeze and Dobson, 233.

[425] Dark, "A Sub-Roman Re-Defense," 113, 115, 120.

[426] Ibid., 119.

[427] Bidwell and Speak, 287.

[428] *RIC* 9.2b (London mint). See Keevill *et al.*, 255.

[429] Dark, "A Sub-Roman Re-Defense," 112, 119.

[430] Ibid.; Johnson, *Hadrian's Wall*, 115; Breeze and Dobson, 231.

[431] Dark, "A Sub-Roman Re-Defense," 112, 119; Breeze and Dobson, 233.

[432] Breeze and Dobson, 234.

[433] Robin Birley, *Civilians on the Roman Frontier* (Newcastle: Graham, 1973), 60.

[434] Dark, "A Sub-Roman Re-Defense," 115, 118.

[435] Ibid., 115.

[436] Wacher, *The Towns*, 136-37.

[437] Todd, *The Coritani*, 140; Laing and Laing, *Celtic Britain*, 76-77; Stafford, *The East MIdlands*, 87. Caedbaed (*Catuboduos*) appears in a genealogy of Aldfrith, an eighth-century English king of Lindsey.

[438] Bede, *EH*, 2.16. Wacher, *The Towns*, 137: "We might wonder if the colonial territorium became one of the protected reserves which seem to have occured in parts of Britain during the earliest part of the Anglo-Saxon period, when an equilibrium was reached between the Romano-British inhabitants of the area and the incoming settlers." Cf. Stafford, *The East Midlands*, 87.

[439] Thomas, *A Provisional List*, 14; Laing and Laing, *Celtic Britain*, 76-77.

[440] Gilmour, "The Anglo-Saxon Church."

[441] Esmonde Cleary, *The Ending*, 152; Todd, *The Coritani*, 140. Stafford (*The East Midlands*, 87) suggests that this sub-Roman Christian community buried their dead on the site of a then-ruined fourth-century church.

[442] Laing, "The Mote of Mark and the Origins of Celtic Interlace."

[443] Radiocarbon calibrations failed to give a more precise date. See Alcock, *Economy*, 241.

[444] Laing, "The Mote of Mark;" Laing and Laing, *Celtic Britain*, 58.

[445] Graham-Campbell *et al.*

[446] Alcock, *Economy*, 241.

[447] Ibid.

[448] Laing and Laing, *Celtic Britain*, 58-59.

[449] Alcock, *Economy*, 241.

[450] Longley, "The Date of the Mote of Mark."

[451] Alcock, *Economy*, 241. Alcock also points out (239) the superstitious awe with which Celtic smiths and craftsmen were regarded in Irish myth, where they often possess their own defended homesteads.

[452] Potter, 45.

[453] Ibid., 366.

[454] Higham and Jones, 128.

[455] Bede, *EH*, 3.4. For discussion on the career of Ninian, see Thomas, *Christianity in Roman Britain*, ch. 11; and MacQueen, *St. Nynia*.

[456] Hill, *Whithorn 4*, 4.

[457] Ibid., 7.

[458] Hill, *Whithorn 2*, 5.

[459] Ibid., 9.

[460] Hill, *Whithorn 4*, 7.

[461] Ibid., 8.

[462] Higham and Jones, *The Carvetii*, 130.

[463] Hill, *Whithorn 4*, 8.

[464] Thomas, *Celtic Britain*, 97. See also Hill, *Whithorn 2*, 4: "None of our sources credit St. Ninian with the conversion of Galloway and we must safely conclude that he was chosen as bishop by a Christian community already in existence."

[465] Thomas, *Celtic Britain*, 99.

[466] Ibid.; Oram, *A Journey Through Time 1*, 12-13; Higham and Jones, 128. Other inscribed stones, dating from the sixth to the twelfth century, have been found at Kirkmadrine and St. Ninian's Cave, a popular early medieval pilgrimage stop.

[467] Alcock, "The North Britons," 136.

[468] Hope-Taylor, *Yeavering*; Alcock, "Gwyr y Gogledd," 6; idem, *Economy*, 242-43.

[469] Hope-Taylor, *Yeavering*, 267.

[470] Ibid., 242 and Fig. 57.

[471] Ibid., 271.

[472] Alcock, *Bede*, 7-8.

[473] Faull, "Settlement and Society," 51.

[474] Welsby, 131.

[475] Wacher, *Towns*, 176; Laing and Laing, *Celtic Britain*, 72.

[476] Campbell, "The Lost Centuries," chapter in *The Anglo-Saxons* (Ithaca, NY: Cornell Univ. Press, 1982), 39.

[477] Bede, *EH*, 1.29.

[478] Ibid., 2.9ff. Cf. *Anglo-Saxon Chronicle* (Laud Chronicle), *sub annum* 626.

GENERAL BIBLIOGRAPHY

I. Bibliographies and Collections.

Allen, J. Romilly and Joseph Anderson. *Early Christian Monuments of Scotland*. Edinburgh: Society of Antiquarians of Scotland, 1903.

Benoit, Fernand. *Sarcophages Paleochrétiens d'Arles et de Marseille, Gallia*. Paris: Centre National de la Recherche Scientifique, 1954.

Bowman, Alan K. and J. David Thomas. *Vindolanda: The Latin Writing-Tablets*. London: Society for the Promotion of Roman Studies, 1983.

British and Irish Archaeology: A Bibliographical Guide. Compiled by A.C. King. Manchester and New York: Manchester Univ. Press, 1994.

Burn, A.R. *The Romans in Britain: An Anthology of Inscriptions*. Columbia, SC: Univ. of South Carolina, 1969.

Collingwood, R.G. and R.P. Wright, eds. *Roman Inscriptions of Britain*. Vol. 1. Oxford: Oxford Univ. Press, 1965.

Goodburn, Roger and Helen Waugh. *Roman Inscriptions of Britain I: Inscriptions on Stone: Epigraphic Indexes*. Gloucester: Sutton, 1983.

Greenstock, M.C., ed. *Some Inscriptions from Roman Britain*. 2nd ed. Hatfield, Hertfordshire: London Association of Classical Teachers, 1971.

Grierson, Philip and Melinda Mays. *Catalogue of Late Roman Coins in the Dumbarton Oaks Collection and in the Whittemore Collection*. Washington, DC: Dumbarton Oaks, 1992.

Ireland, S. *Roman Britain: A Sourcebook*. London and New York: Routledge, 1986.

MacAlister, R.A.S. *Corpus Inscriptionum Insularum Celticarum*. Vol. 1. Dublin: Stationery Office, 1945.

Mann, J.C., ed. *The Northern Frontier in Britain from Hadrian to Honorius: Literary and Epigraphic Sources*. Newcastle upon Tyne: Museum of Antiquities, 1969.

Mattingly, Harold *et al.*, eds. *Roman Imperial Coinage*. 10 vols. London: Spink, 1923-94.

Nash-Williams, V.E. *The Early Christian Monuments of Wales*. Cardiff: Univ. of Wales Press, 1950.

Robertson, Anne S. *Roman Imperial Coins in the Hunter Coin Cabinet, University of Glasgow*. Oxford: Oxford Univ. Press, 1982.

II. Secondary Sources.

(Note: Excavation reports are listed under the individual sites in the Gazetteer.)

Abrams, Leslie and James P. Carley, eds. *The Archaeology and History of Glastonbury Abbey. Essays in Honor of the Ninetieth Birthday of C.A. Ralegh Radford*. Woodbridge, Suffolk: Boydell, 1991.

Alcock, Elizabeth A. "Appendix: Defended Settlements, Fifth to Seventh Centuries AD." In *25 Years of Medieval Archaeology*, ed. D. Hinton, pp. 58-59. Sheffield: Univ. of Sheffield Press, 1983.

—. "Appendix: Enclosed Places, AD 500-800." In *Power and Politics*, ed. S.T. Driscoll and M.R. Nieke, pp. 40-46. Edinburgh: Edinburgh Univ. Press, 1988.

Alcock, Leslie. "'By South Cadbury is that Camelot....'" *Antiquity* 41 (1967): 50-53.

—. "Was There an Irish Sea Culture-Province in the Dark Ages?" In *The Irish Sea Province*, ed. D. Moore, pp. 55-65. Cardiff: Cambrian Archaeological Association, 1970.

—. *Arthur's Britain*. New York: Penguin, 1971.

—. *'By South Cadbury is that Camelot.'* London: Thames and Hudson, 1972.

—. "Refortified or Newly Fortified? The Chronology of Dinas Powys." *Antiquity* 54 (1980): 231-32.

—. "The Cadbury Castle Sequence in the First Millennium BC." *BBCS* 28 (1980): 656-718.

—. "Cadbury-Camelot: a Fifteen-Year Perspective." *Proceedings of the British Academy* 68 (1982): 355-88.

—. "Gwyr y Gogledd: An Archaeological Appraisal." *Archaeologia Cambrensis* 132 (1983): 1-18.

—. "The Archaeology of Celtic Britain, Fifth to Twelfth Centuries AD," in *Twenty Five Years of Medieval Archaeology*, ed. D.A. Hinton, pp. 48-66. Sheffield: Dept. of Prehistory and Archaeology, Univ. of Sheffield, 1983.

—. *Economy, Society and Warfare Among the Britons and Saxons*. Cardiff: Univ. of Wales Press, 1987.

—. "The Activities of Potentates in Celtic Britain, AD 500-800: A Positivist Approach." In *Power and Politics in Early Medieval Britain and Ireland*, ed. S.T. Driscoll and M.R. Nieke, pp. 22-46. Edinburgh: Edinburgh Univ. Press, 1988.

—. *Bede, Eddius and the Forts of the North Britons*. Jarrow Lecture, 1988.

Alcock, Leslie and Geoffrey Ashe. "Cadbury: is it Camelot?" In *The Quest for Arthur's Britain*, ed. Geoffrey Ashe, pp. 123-47. London: Paladin Press, 1968.

Allason-Jones, Lindsay. *Women in Roman Britain*. London: British Museum Publications, 1989.

Applebaum, Shimon. "Land Tenure and Politics in Fifth-Century Britain," in *The Romano-British Countryside*, ed. D. Miles, pp. 433-49. BAR British Series No. 103. Oxford, 1982.

Arnold, C.J. "The End of Roman Britain: Some Discussion," in *The Romano-British Countryside*, ed. D. Miles, pp. 451-59. BAR British Series No. 103. Oxford, 1982.

—. *Roman Britain to Saxon England*. Bloomington, IN: Indiana Univ. Press, 1984.

Ashe, Geoffrey, ed. *The Quest for Arthur's Britain*. London: Paladin, 1971.

Barker, P.A. *et al.* "Two Burials Under the Refectory at Worcester Cathedral." *Medieval Archaeology* 18 (1974): 146-51.

Barker, Philip, ed. *From Roman 'Viroconium' to Medieval Wroxeter*. Worcester: West Mercian Archaeological Consultants, Ltd., 1990.

Barley, M.W. and R.P.C. Hanson, eds. *Christianty in Britain, 300-700*. Leicester: Leicester Univ. Press, 1968.

Bassett, Steven. "Churches in Worcester Before and After the Anglo-Saxons." *Antiquaries Jrnl* 69 (1989): 225-56.

—. "In Search of the Origins of Anglo-Saxon Kingdoms." In

The Origins of Anglo-Saxon Kingdoms, ed. S. Bassett, pp. 3-27. Leicester: Leicester Univ. Press, 1989.

—. "Church and Diocese in the West Midlands: The Transition from British to Anglo-Saxon Control," in *Pastoral Care Before the Parish*, ed. J. Blair and R. Sharpe, pp. 13-40. Leicester: Leicester Univ. Press, 1992.

Bassett, Steven, ed. *The Origins of the Anglo-Saxon Kingdoms*. Leicester: Leicester Univ. Press, 1989.

Beacham, Peter *et al*. *Archaeology of the Devon Landscape*. Exeter: Devon County Council, 1980.

Bell, M. *Brean Down Excavations 1983-87*. London: English Heritage, 1990.

Biddle, Martin. "The Study of Winchester: Archaeology and History in a British Town." *Proceedings of the British Academy* 69 (1983): 93-135.

Biddle, Martin and Birthe Kjølbye-Biddle. *The Origins of Saint Albans Abbey: Excavations in the Cloister 1982-1983*. St. Albans, Hertfordshire: St. Albans Abbey Research Committee, 1984.

Bidwell, Paul T. *The Roman Fort of Vindolanda at Chesterholm, Northumberland*. London: Historic Buildings and Monuments Commission, 1985.

Birley, Anthony R. *The People of Roman Britain*. Berkeley, CA: Univ. of Cal. Press, 1980.

—. *The 'Fasti' of Roman Britain*. Oxford: Clarendon Press, 1981.

Birley, Robin. *Civilians on the Roman Frontier*. Newcastle: Graham, 1973.

—. "Vindolanda." *Current Archaeology* 116 (1989): 275-79.

Blackburn, M. "Three Silver Coins in the Names of Valentinian III (425-55) and Anthemius (467-72) from Chatham Lines, Kent." *Numismatic Chronicle* 148 (1988): 169-74.

Blagg, T.F.C. and A.C. King, eds. *Military and Civilian in Roman Britain*. BAR British Series No. 136. Oxford, 1984.

Boon, George C. *Silchester: The Roman Town of Calleva*. London: David and Charles, 1974.

—. *The Roman Town 'Calleva Atrebatum' at Silchester, Hampshire*. Reading: Calleva Museum, 1983.

—. "Theodosian Coins from North and South Wales." *BBCS* 33 (1986): 429-35.

—. "Counterfeit Coins in Roman Britain." In *Coins and the Archaeologist*, ed. J. Casey and R. Reece, pp. 102-88. London: Seaby, 1987.

Bowen, E.G. "Britain and the British Seas," in *The Irish Sea Province*, ed. D. Moore, pp. 13-28. Cardiff: Cambrian Archaeological Association, 1970.

Bowman, Alan K. *The Roman Writing Tablets from Vindolanda*. London: British Museum Publications, 1983.

Branigan, Keith. *Town and Country: the Archaeology of Verulamium and the Roman Chilterns*. Bourne End, Buckinghamshire: Spurbooks, 1973.

—. *The Catuvellauni*. Gloucester: Sutton, 1985.

Breeze, David J. *The Northern Frontiers of Roman Britain*. New York: St. Martin's, 1982.

Breeze, David J. and Brian Dobson. "Roman Military Deployment in North England." *Britannia* 16 (1985): 1-19.

—. *Hadrian's Wall*. 3rd ed. London: Penguin, 1987.

Brickstock, R.J. *Copies of the Fel Temp Reparatio Coinage in Britain: A Study of Their Chronology and Archaeological Significance Including Gazetteers of Hoards and Site Finds*. BAR British Series No. 176. Oxford, 1987.

Bromwich, Rachel *et al*., eds. *The Arthur of the Welsh: The Arthurian Legend in Medieval Welsh Literature*. Cardiff: Univ. of Wales Press, 1991.

Brooke, C.N.L. *et al*., eds. *Studies in Numismatic Method Presented to Philip Grierson*. Cambridge: Cambridge Univ. Press, 1983.

Brooks, Dodie A. "A Review of the Evidence for Continuity in British Towns in the Fifth and Sixth Centuries." *Oxford Journal of Archaeology* 5, no. 1 (1986): 77-102.

Burkitt, F.C. and L.C.G. Clarke. "Roman Pewter Bowl from the Isle of Ely." *Proceedings of the Cambridge Antiquarian Society* 31 (1931): 66-72.

Burnett, Andrew. "Clipped *Siliquae* and the End of Roman Britain." *Britannia* 15 (1984): 163-68.

Burnham, Barry C. and John Wacher. *The 'Small Towns' of Roman Britain*. London: B.T. Batsford, 1990.

Burnham, B.C. and J.L. Davies, eds. *Conquest, Co-Existence and Change*. Lampeter, Dyfed: St. David's Univ. College, 1990.

Burns, Thomas S. and Bernhard H. Overbeck. *Rome and the Germans as Seen in Coinage: Catalog for the Exhibition*. Atlanta, GA: Emory Univ., 1987.

Burrow, Ian. "Tintagel—Some Problems." *Scottish Archaeological Forum* 5 (1973): 99-103.

—. "Dark Age Devon: The Landscape AD 400-1100." In *Archaeology of the Devon Landscape*, ed. Peter Beacham *et al*. Exeter: Devon County Council, 1980.

—. *Hillfort and Hill-Top Settlement in Somerset in the First to Eighth Centuries AD*. BAR British Series No. 91. Oxford: BAR Publishing, 1981.

—. Review of *Economy, Society, and Warfare*, by Leslie Alcock. In *Antiquity* 61 (1987): 494-95.

Campbell, Ewan. "Coygan Camp." In *Early Medieval Settlements in Wales AD 400-1100*, ed. N. Edwards and A. Lane, pp. 44-46. Cardiff: Univ. of Wales, 1988.

—. "Dinas Emrys." In *Early Medieval Settlements in Wales AD 400-1100*, ed. N. Edwards and A. Lane, pp. 54-57. Cardiff: Univ. of Wales, 1988.

Campbell, Ewan and Alan Lane. "Excavations at Longbury Bank, Dyfed." *Medieval Archaeology* 37 (1993): 15-17.

Campbell, James, ed. *The Anglo-Saxons*. Ithaca, NY: Cornell Univ. Press, 1982.

Casey, P.J. "Constantine the Great in Britain—the evidence of the coinage at the London mint." In *Collectanea Londiniensia*, ed. J. Bird, H. Chapman, and J. Clark, pp. 181-93. London and Middlesex Archaeological Society Special Paper No. 2. London: London and Middlesex Archaeological Society, 1978.

—. *Roman Coinage in Britain*. Aylesbury: Shire Archaeology, 1980.

Casey, P.J., ed. *The End of Roman Britain*. BAR British Series No. 71. Oxford: BAR Publishing, 1979.

Casey, P.J. and Richard Reece. *Coins and the Archaeologist*. 2nd ed. London: Seaby, 1988.

Collingwood, R.G. *The Archaeology of Roman Britain.* New York: Dial Press, 1930.

Collingwood, R.G. and J.N.L. Myres. *Roman Britain and the English Settlements.* Oxford: Clarendon Press, 1936.

Corbishley, Mike. *Town Life in Roman Britain.* London: Harrap, 1981.

Crickmore, J. *Romano-British Urban Settlements in the West Midlands.* BAR British Series No. 127. Oxford: BAR Publishing, 1984.

Crow, J.G. *Housesteads Roman Fort.* London: English Heritage, 1989.

Cruden, Stewart. *Early Christian and Pictish Monuments.* London: HMSO, 1964.

Cunliffe, Barry. *The Regni.* London: Duckworth, 1973.

—. *Excavations at Portchester Castle, Vol. I: Roman.* Society of Antiquaries Research Report No. 32. London: Society of Antiquaries, 1975.

—. *Excavations at Portchester Castle, Vol. II: Saxon.* Society of Antiquaries Research Report No. 33. London: Society of Antiquaries, 1976.

—. *The Celtic World.* New York: Crown, 1986.

Cunliffe, Barry and Peter Davenport. *The Temple of Sulis Minerva at Bath: Vol. 1, The Site.* Oxford: Oxford Univ. Committee for Archaeology, 1985.

Dark, Kenneth Rainsbury. "Celtic Monastic Archaeology: Fifth to Eighth Centuries." *Monastic Studies* 14 (1983): 17-30.

—. "The Plan and Interpretaion of Tintagel." *CMCS* 9 (1985): 1-17.

—. "High Status Sites, Kingship, and State Formation in Post-Roman Western Britain AD 400-700." Ph.D. Thesis, Cambridge Univ., 1989.

—. "A Sub-Roman Re-Defense of Hadrian's Wall?" *Britannia* 23 (1992): 111-20.

—. *The Inscribed Stones of Dyfed.* Llandysul, Dyfed: Gomer Press, 1992.

—. "St. Patrick's *Uillula* and the Fifth-Century Occupation of Romano-British Villas." In *Saint Patrick*, D. Dumville et al., pp. 19-24. Woodbridge, Suffolk: Boydell, 1993.

—. *Civitas to Kingdom: British Political Continuity 300-800.* Leicester: Leicester Univ. Press, 1993.

—. *Discovery by Design: The Identification of Secular Elite Settlements in Western Britain AD 400-700.* BAR British Series No. 237. Oxford: BAR Publishing, 1994.

Darling, M.J. "The Caistor-By-Norwich 'Massacre' Reconsidered." *Britannia* 18 (1987): 263-72.

Davies, K. Rutherford. *Britons and Saxons. The Chiltern Region.* Chichester: Phillimore, 1982.

Davies, Wendy. "*Unciae*: Land Measurement in the *Liber Landavensis.*" *Agrarian History Review* 21 (1973): 115-17.

—. *An Early Welsh Microcosm: Studies in the Llandaff Charters.* London: Royal Historical Society, 1978.

—. *Wales in the Early Middle Ages.* Leicester: Leicester Univ. Press, 1982.

—. "A Historian's View of Celtic Archaeology." In *Twenty Five Years of Medieval Archaeology*, ed. D.A. Hinton, pp. 67-73. Sheffield: Dept. of Prehistory and Archaeology, Univ. of Sheffield, 1983.

De La Bédoyère, Guy. *The Finds of Roman Britain.* London: Batsford, 1989.

—. *The Buildings of Roman Britain.* London: Batsford, 1991.

Detsicas, Alec. *The Cantiaci.* Gloucester: Sutton, 1983.

Detsicas, Alec, ed. *Collectanea Historica: Essays in Memory of Stuart Rigold.* Gloucester: Sutton, 1981.

Dixon, Philip. "'The cities are not populated as once they were.'" In *The City in Late Antiquity*, ed. J. Rich, pp. 145-60. London: Routledge, 1992.

Dore, J.N. *Corbridge Roman Site.* London: English Heritage, 1989.

Dore, J. and K. Greene, eds. *Roman Pottery Studies in Britain and Beyond.* BAR Supplemental Series No. 30. Oxford: BAR Publishing, 1977.

Down, Alec. *Roman Chichester.* Chichester: Phillimore, 1988.

Drinkwater, John and Hugh Elton, eds. *Fifth-Century Gaul: A Crisis of Identity?* Cambridge: Cambridge Univ. Press, 1992.

Driscoll, S.T. and M.R. Nieke, eds. *Power and Politics in Early Medieval Britain and Ireland.* Edinburgh: Edinburgh Univ. Press, 1988.

Drury, P.J. "Chelmsford." *Current Archaeology* 41 (1974): 166-76.

Dumville, David N. et al. *Saint Patrick, AD 493-1993.* Woodbridge, Suffolk: Boydell, 1993.

Dunnett, Rosalind. *The Trinovantes.* London: Duckworth, 1975.

Edwards, Nancy and Alan Lane, eds. *Early Medieval Settlements in Wales 400-1100.* Cardiff: Univ. of Wales Press, 1988.

—. *The Early Church in Wales and the West.* Oxbow Monograph No. 16. Oxford: Oxbow, 1992.

Ellison, Ann. *Excavations at West Hill Uley: 1977-79. A Native, Roman and Christian Ritual Complex of the First Millenium AD—Second Interim Report.* Bristol: Committee for Rescue Archaeology in Avon, Gloucestershire and Somerset, 1980.

Esmonde Cleary, A.S. *Extra-Mural Areas of Romano-British Towns.* BAR British Series No. 169. Oxford: BAR Publishing, 1987.

—. *The Ending of Roman Britain.* London: Batsford, 1989.

Evans, Jeremy. "Towns and the End of Roman Britain in Northern England." *Scottish Archaeological Review* 2 (1983): 144-49.

—. "From the End of Roman Britain to the Celtic West." *Oxford Journal of Archaeology* 9 (1990): 91-103.

Evison, Vera I. *The Fifth-Century Invasions South of the Thames.* London: Athlone Press, 1965.

Evison, Vera, ed. *Angles, Saxons, and Jutes.* Oxford: Clarendon Press, 1981.

Faull, Margaret L. "British Survival in Anglo-Saxon Northumbria." In *Studies in Celtic Sruvival*, ed. L. Laing, pp. 1-56. BAR No. 37. Oxford: BAR Publishing, 1977.

—. "British Survival in Anglo-Saxon Yorkshire." Unpubl. Ph.D. Thesis, Leeds University, 1979.

—. "Settlement and Society in North-East England in the Fifth Century." In *Settlement and Society in the Roman North*, ed. P.R. Wilson et al., pp. 49-52. Bradford, West Yorkshire: Yorkshire Archaeological

Society, 1984.

Frend, W.H.C. "Pagans, Christians, and 'the Barbarian Conspiracy' of AD 367 in Roman Britain." *Britannia* 23 (1992): 121-31.

Frere, Sheppard. *Britannia: A History of Roman Britain.* London: Routledge and Kegan Paul, 1967.

—. *Verulamium Excavations (1972-84).* Vols. 1-3. London: Society of Antiquaries, 1983.

Frere, S.S. and J.K.S. St. Joseph. *Roman Britain from the Air.* Cambridge: Cambridge Univ. Press, 1983.

Frere, S.S. et al. "Roman Britain in 1987." *Britannia* 19 (1988): 416-84 (477).

Friell, J.G.P. and W.G. Watson, eds. *Pictish Studies: Settlement, Burial and Art in Dark Age Northern Britain.* BAR British Series No. 125. Oxford, 1984.

Fulford, Michael G. "Pottery and Britain's Foreign Trade in the Later Roman Period." In *Pottery and Early Commerce: Characterization and Trade in Roman and Later Ceramics*, ed. D.P.S. Peacock, pp. 35-84. London/New York/San Francisco: Academic Press, 1977.

—. "Silchester." *Current Archaeology* 82 (1982): 326-31.

—. *Silchester Defenses 1974-80.* Britannia Monograph Series No. 5. London: Society for the Promotion of Roman Studies, 1984.

—. "Excavations on the Sites of the Amphitheatre and Forum-Basilica at Silchester, Hampshire: an Interim Report." *Antiquaries Journal* 65 (1985): 39-81.

—. *Guide to the Silchester Excavations: The Forum Basilica 1982-84.* Reading: Reading Univ. Press, 1985.

—. *The Silchester Amphitheatre: Excavations of 1979-85.* Britannia Monograph Series No. 10. London: Society for the Promotion of Roman Studies, 1989.

—. "Byzantium and Britain." *Medieval Archaeology* 33 (1989): 1-5.

Galliou, Patrick and Michael Jones. *The Bretons.* Oxford: Blackwell, 1991.

Gelling, Margaret. *The West Midlands in the Early Middle Ages.* Leicester: Leicester Univ. Press, 1992.

Gilchrist, Roberta. "A Re-appraisal of Dinas Powys." *Medieval Archaeology* 32 (1988): 50-62.

Goodburn, Roger and Philip Bartholomew, eds. *Aspects of the 'Notitia Dignitatum.'* BAR Supplemental Series No. 15. Oxford, 1976.

Greep, Stephen J., ed. *Roman Towns: The Wheeler Inheritance: A Review of 50 Years' Research.* CBA Research Report No. 93. York: CBA, 1993.

Guilbert, Graeme, ed. *Hill-Fort Studies: Essays for A.H.A. Hogg.* Leicester: Leicester Univ. Press, 1981.

Hanley, Robin. *Villages in Roman Britain.* Aylesbury: Shire Archaeology, 1987.

Hartley, B.R. and R. Leon Fitts. *The Brigantes.* Gloucester: Sutton, 1988.

Haselgrove, Susanne. "Romano-Saxon Attitudes." In *The End of Roman Britain*, ed. P.J. Casey, pp.4-13. BAR British Series No. 71. Oxford: 1979.

Hawkes, S.C. and G.C. Dunning. "Soldiers and Settlers in Britain, Fourth to Fifth Century." *Medieval Archaeology* 5 (1961): 1-70.

Hayes, John. *Late Roman Pottery.* London: British School at Rome, 1972.

Henderson, Isabel. *The Picts.* New York: Praeger, 1967.

Henig, Martin. *Religion in Roman Britain.* London: B.T. Batsford, 1984.

Higgitt, J. *Early Medieval Sculpture in Britain and Ireland.* BAR British Series No. 152. Oxford, 1986.

Higham, Nicholas. *The Northern Counties to AD 1000.* London: Longman, 1986.

—. "Gildas, Roman Walls, and British Dykes." *CMCS* 22 (1991): 1-14.

—. *Rome, Britain and the Anglo-Saxons.* London: Seaby, 1992.

—. *The Kingdom of Northumbria AD 350-1100.* Gloucester: Sutton, 1993.

Higham, Nicholas and Barri Jones. *The Carvetii.* Gloucester: Sutton, 1985.

Hill, Peter. *Whithorn 2: Excavations 1984-7, Interim Report.* Whithorn: Whithorn Trust, 1988.

—. *Whithorn 3: Excavations 1988-90, Interim Report.* Whithorn: Whithorn Trust, 1990.

—. *Whithorn 4: Excavations 1990-1, Interim Report.* Whithorn: Whithorn Trust, 1992.

Hills, Catherine. "Review of *Rome, Britain and the Anglo-Saxons* by N. Higham." In *Antiquity* 66 (1992): 988-99.

Hines, John. "Philology, Archaeology and the *Adventus Saxonum vel Anglorum*." In *Britain 400-600*, ed. A. Bammesberger and A. Wollmann, pp. 17-36. Heidelberg: C. Winter, 1990.

Hingley, Richard. *Rural Settlement in Roman Britain.* London: Seaby, 1989.

Hinton, David A., ed. *Twenty Five Years of Medieval Archaeology.* Sheffield: Dept. of Prehistory and Archaeology, Univ. of Sheffield, 1983.

Hodges, Richard. *The Anglo-Saxon Achievement: Archaeology and the Beginnings of English Society.* London: Duckworth, 1989.

Holbrook, Neil and Paul T. Bidwell, eds. *Exeter Archaeological Reports: Vol. IV, Roman Finds from Exeter.* Exeter: Exeter Univ. Press, 1991.

Hope-Taylor, Brian. *Yeavering: An Anglo-British Centre of Early Northumbria.* London: HMSO, 1977.

—. "Balbride . . . and Doon Hill." *Current Archaeology* 72 (1980): 18-19

Hurst, H.R. *Gloucester, The Roman and Later Defenses.* Gloucester: Archaeological Publications, 1986.

Jackson, Kenneth. *Language and History in Early Britain.* Edinburgh: Edinburgh Univ. Press, 1953.

James, Edward. "The Origins of Barbarian Kingdoms; the Continental Evidence." In *The Origins of Anglo-Saxon Kingdoms*, ed. Steven Bassett. Leicester: Leicester Univ. Press, 1989.

James, Heather. "Early Medieval Cemeteries in Wales." In *The Early Church in Wales and the West*, ed. N. Edwards and A. Lane, pp. 90-103. Oxbow Monograph No. 16. Oxford: Oxbow, 1992.

Johns, C.M. and T.W. Potter. "The Canterbury Late Roman Treasure." *Antiquaries Journal* 55 (1985): 313-52.

Johnson, Stephen. *The Roman Forts of the Saxon Shore*. London: Paul Elek, 1976.

—. *Later Roman Britain*. London: Paladin, 1986.

Johnston, D.E., ed. *The Saxon Shore*. London: Council for British Archaeology, 1977.

Jones, Barri and David Mattingly. *An Atlas of Roman Britain*. Oxford: Blackwell, 1990.

Jones, Michael E. "Provinces of Iron and Rust: The End of Roman Britain." Unpubl. Ph.D. Dissertation, Univ. of Texas at Austin, 1985.

Jones, Myfanwy Lloyd. *Society and Settlement in Wales and the Marches (500 BC to AD 1100)*. 2 vols. BAR British Series No. 121. Oxford, 1984.

Keay, Simon. *Late Roman Amphorae in the Western Mediterranean*. 2 vols. BAR International Series No. 196. Oxford, 1984.

Kelly, Richard S. "Recent Research on the Hut Group Settlements of North-West Wales." In *Conquest, Co-Existence and Change*, ed. B. Burnham and J. Davies, pp. 102-11. Lampeter, Dyfed: St. David's Univ. College, 1990.

Kent, J.P.C. "The End of Roman Britain: The Literary and Numismatic Evidence Reviewed." In *The End of Roman Britain*, ed. P.J. Casey, pp. 15-27. BAR British Series No. 71. Oxford, 1979.

Knight, Jeremy K. "*In Tempore Iustini Consulis*: Contacts Between the British and Gaulish Churches Before Augustine." In *Collectanea Historica*, ed. A. Detsicas, pp. 54-62. Gloucester: Sutton, 1981.

Knight, J. et al. "New Finds of Early Christian Monuments." *Archaeologia Cambrensis* 126 (1977): 60-73.

Knight, J.K. and Alan Lane. "Caerwent." In *Early Medieval Settlements in Wales*, ed. N. Edwards and A. Lane, pp. 35-38. Cardiff: Univ. of Wales, 1988

Laing, Lloyd. *Settlement Types in Post-Roman Scotland*. BAR No. 13. Oxford: BAR Publishing, 1975.

—. "Segontium and the Roman Occupation of Wales." In *Studies in Celtic Survival*, pp. 57-60. BAR No. 37. Oxford, 1977.

—. "The Beginnings of 'Dark Age' Celtic Art." In *Britain 400-600*, ed. A. Bammesberger and A. Wollmann, pp. 37-50. Heidelberg: C. Winter, 1990.

Laing, Lloyd, ed. *Studies in Celtic Survival*. BAR No. 37. Oxford, 1977.

Laing, Lloyd and Jennifer. *The Dark Ages of West Cheshire*. Chester Council Monograph Series No. 6. Chester: City Council, 1986.

—. *Celtic Britain and Ireland AD 200-800: The Myth of the Dark Ages*. New York: St. Martin's, 1990.

Lane, Allan. "Degannwy Castle." In *Early Medieval Settlements in Wales*, ed. N. Edwards and A. Lane, pp. 50-53. Cardiff: Univ. of Wales, 1988.

Leach, Peter. *Shepton Mallet: Romano-Britons and Early Christians in Somerset*. Birmingham: Birmingham University Field Archaeology Unit, 1991.

McWhirr, Alan. "Cirencester—'Corinium Dobunnorum.'" In *Roman Towns: The Wheeler Inheritance*, ed. S. Greep, pp. 46-49. CBA Report No. 93. York: CBA, 1993.

McWhirr, Alan, ed. *Studies in the Archaeology and History of Cirencester*. BAR No. 30. Oxford: BAR Publishing, 1976.

MacMullen, Ramsay. *Soldier and Civilian in the Later Roman Empire*. Cambridge, MA: Harvard Univ. Press, 1963.

MacQueen, J. *St. Nynia*. Edinburgh: Polygon, 1990.

Mann, J.C. "Epigraphic Consciousness." *Journal of Roman Studies* 75 (1985): 204-6.

Maxfield, Valerie A., ed. *The Saxon Shore: A Handbook*. Exeter: Exeter Univ. Press, 1989.

Maxfield, V.A. and M.J. Dobson. *Roman Frontier Studies 1989*. Exeter: Exeter Univ. Press, 1991.

Mays, Melinda. *Celtic Coinage: Britain and Beyond. The Eleventh Oxford Symposium on Coinage and Monetary History*. BAR British Series No. 222. Oxford: BAR Publishing, 1992.

Miles, David, ed. *The Romano-British Countryside: Studies in Rural Settlement and Economy*. BAR British Series No. 103. Oxford: BAR Publishing, 1982.

Millet, Martin. *The Romanization of Britain*. Cambridge: Cambridge Univ. Press, 1990.

Milne, Gustav. "The Rise and Fall of Roman London." In *Roman Towns: The Wheeler Inheritance*, ed. S. Greep, pp. 11-15. CBA Report No. 93. York: CBA, 1993.

Moore, Donald, ed. *The Irish Sea Province in Archaeology and History*. Cardiff: Cambrian Archaeological Association, 1970.

Morris, C.D. "Tintagel Castle Excavations 1990." Unpubl. interim statement, Univ. of Durham, 1990.

—. "Tintagel Island 1990, an Interim Report." *Cornish Archaeology* 30 (1991): 260-62.

Morris, C.D. et al. "Tintagel, Cornwall: The 1990 Excavations." *Antiquity* 64 (1990): 843-49.

Morris, Richard. *The Church in British Archaeology*. CBA Research Report No. 47. London: CBA, 1983.

—. *Churches in the Landscape*. London: Dent, 1989.

Musset, Lucien. *The Germanic Invasions*. Trans. by Edward and Columba James. Univ. Park, PA: Penn. State Univ. Press, 1975.

Musson, C.R. et al. *The Breiddin Hillfort. A Later Prehistoric Settlement in the Welsh Marches*. CBA Report No. 76. London: CBA, 1991.

Myres, J.N.L. "Pelagius and the End of Roman Rule in Britain." *Journal of Roman Studies* (1960): 21-50.

—. *The English Settlements*. Oxford: Clarendon Press, 1986.

Neal, David S. *Lullingstone Roman Villa*. London: English Heritage, 1991.

Niblett, Rosalind. "'Verulamium' since the Wheelers." In *Roman Towns: The Wheeler Inheritance*, ed. S. Greep, pp. 78-92. CBA Report No. 93. York: CBA, 1993.

Nowakowski, Jaqueline A., and Charles Thomas. *Excavations at Tintagel Parish Churchyard: Interim Report, Spring 1990*. Truro: Institute of Cornish Studies, 1990.

—. *Grave News from Tintagel. An Account of a Second Season of Archaeological Excavation at Tintagel Churchyard, Cornwall*. Truro: Institute of Cornish Studies, 1992.

Olson, Lynette. *Early Monasteries in Cornwall*. Woodbridge, Suffolk: Boydell, 1989.

Oram, R.D. *A Journey Through Time 1: The Christian Heritage of Wigtownshire*. Whithorn: Whithorn Trust, 1987.

—. *A Journey Through Time 2: The Archaeology of Wigtownshire*. Whithorn: Whithorn Trust, 1987.

Ottaway, Patrick. *Archaeology in British Towns: From Emperor Claudius to the Black Death*. London: Routledge, 1992.

Padel, O.J. "Tintagel—An Alternative View." In *A Provisional List of Imported Pottery in Post-Roman Western Britain and Ireland*, Charles Thomas, pp. 28-29. Truro: Institute of Cornish Studies, 1981.

—. "Some Southwestern Sites with Arthurian Associations." In *The Arthur of the Welsh*, ed. R. Bromwich et al., pp. 229-48. Cardiff: Univ. of Wales Press, 1991.

Peacock, D.P.S. *Amphorae and the Roman Economy*. London: Longman, 1986.

Peacock, D.P.S., ed. *Pottery and Early Commerce: Characterization and Trade in Roman and Later Ceramics*. London/New York/San Francisco: Academic Press, 1977.

Pearce, Susan M. *The Kingdom of Dumnonia*. Padstow, Cornwall: Lodenek Press, 1978.

—. "Estates and Church Sites in Dorset and Gloucestershire: The Emergence of a Christian Society." In *The Early Church in Western Britain and Ireland*, ed. S. Pearce, pp. 117-38. BAR British Series No. 102. Oxford, 1982.

Pearce, Susan, ed. *The Early Church in Western Britain and Ireland*. BAR British Series No. 102. Oxford: BAR Publishing, 1982.

Percival, J. *The Roman Villa*. London: Batsford, 1976.

—. "Fifth-Century Villas: New Life or Death Postponed?" In *Fifth-Century Gaul*, ed. J. Drinkwater and H. Elton, pp. 156-64. Cambridge: Cambridge Univ. Press, 1992.

Pierce, G.O. *The Place-Names of Dinas Powys Hundred*. Cardiff: Univ. of Wales Press, 1968.

Potter, T.W. *Romans in North-West England*. Kendal, Cumbria: T. Wilson, 1979.

Quinnell, Henrietta. "Cornwall During the Iron Age and Roman Period." *Cornish Archaeology* 25 (1986): 111-34.

Radford, C.A.R. *Tintagel Castle*. London: Historic Buildings and Monuments Commission, 1939.

—. "Imported Pottery Found at Tintagel, Cornwall." In *Dark Age Britain*, ed. D.B. Harden, pp. 59-67. London: Methuen, 1956.

—. "Romance and Reality in Cornwall." In *The Quest for Arthur's Britain*, ed. Geoffrey Ashe, pp. 59-77. New York: Paladin, 1971.

—. "Glastonbury Abbey." In *The Quest for Arthur's Britain*, ed. Geoffrey Ashe, pp. 97-110. New York: Paladin, 1971.

Radford, C.A.R. and Michael J. Swanton. *Arthurian Sites in the West*. Exeter: Exeter Univ. Press, 1975.

Rahtz, Philip. "Excavations on Glastonbury Tor, Somerset, 1964-66." *Archaeological Journal* 127 (1970): 1-81.

—. "Glastonbury Tor." In *The Quest for Arthur's Britain*, ed. Geoffrey Ashe, pp. 111-22. New York: Paladin Press, 1971.

Rahtz, Philip et al. *Cadbury Congresbury 1968-73: A Late/Post-Roman Hilltop Settlement in Somerset*. BAR British Series No. 223. Oxford: BAR Publishing, 1992.

Ramm, Herman. *The Parisi*. London: Duckworth, 1978.

Reece, Richard M. "Town and Country: The End of Roman Britain." *World Archaeology* 12 (1980): 77-92.

—. "The End of Roman Britain—Revisited." *Scottish Archaeological Review* 2 (1983): 149-53.

—. "The Use of Roman Coinage." *Oxford Journal of Archaeology* 3 (1984): 197-210.

—. "Mints, Markets and the Military." In *Military and Civilian in Roman Britain*, ed. T.F. Blagg and A.C. King, pp. 143-60. BAR British Series No. 136. Oxford, 1984.

—. *Coinage in Roman Britain*. London: Seaby, 1987.

—. *My Roman Britain*. Cirencester: Cotswold Studies Vol. 3, 1988.

—. "The End of the City in Roman Britain." In *The City in Late Antiquity*, ed. J. Rich, pp. 136-44. London: Routledge, 1992.

Reece, Richard and Christopher Catling. *Cirencester: The Development and Buildings of a Cotswold Town*. BAR No. 12. Oxford, 1975.

Renfrew, Colin. *Archaeology and Language*. London: Cape, 1987.

Renfrew, A.C. and S.J. Shennan, eds. *Ranking Resource and Exchange*. Cambridge: Cambridge Univ. Press, 1982.

Reynolds, Nicholas. "Dark Age Timber Halls and the Background to Excavation at Balbridie." *Scottish Archaeological Forum* 10 (1980): 41-60.

Rich, John, ed. *The City in Late Antiquity*. London: Routledge, 1992.

Ritchie, Anna. *The Picts*. Edinburgh: HMSO, 1989.

Rivet, A.L.F., ed. *The Roman Villa in Britain*. New York: Praeger, 1969.

Rivet, A.L.F. and Colin Smith. *The Place-Names of Roman Britain*. Princeton, NJ: Princeton Univ. Press, 1979.

Robertson, Anne S. "Romano-British Coin Hoards: Their Numismatic, Archaeological and Historical Significance." In *Coins and the Archaeologist*, ed. P.J. Casey and R. Reece, pp. 13-37. London: Seaby, 1988.

Rodwell, Warwick and Trevor Rowley, eds. *The 'Small Towns' of Roman Britain*. BAR No. 15. Oxford, 1975.

Salway, Peter. *The Frontier People of Roman Britain*. Cambridge: Cambridge Univ. Press, 1965.

—. *Roman Britain*. Oxford: Oxford Univ. Press, 1984.

—. *The Oxford Illustrated History of Roman Britain*. Oxford: Oxford Univ. Press, 1993.

Sharples, Niall M. *Maiden Castle*. London: Batsford/English Heritage, 1991.

Shennan, Stephen, ed. *Archaeological Approaches to Cultural Identity*. London: Unwin Hyman, 1989.

Simpson, C.J. "Belt-Buckles and Strap-Ends of the Later Roman Empire." *Britannia* 7 (1976): 192-223.

Smith, Lesley M., ed. *The Making of Britain: The Dark Ages*. London: Macmillan, 1984.

Smyth, Alfred P. *Warlords and Holy Men: Scotland AD 80-1000*. London: Edward Arnold, 1984.

Snyder, Christopher A. "'The Tyrants of Tintagel': The Terminology and Archaeology of Sub-Roman Britain (AD 400-600)." Ph.D.diss., Emory University, 1994.

—. *An Age of Tyrants: Britain, AD 400-600*. Univ. Park, PA: Penn State Univ. Press, forthcoming.

Sorrell, Alan. *Roman Towns in Britain*. London: Batsford, 1976.

Stafford, Pauline. *The East Midlands in the Early Middle Ages*. Leicester: Leicester Univ. Press, 1985.

Steer, K.A. "Two Unrecorded Early Christian Stones." *PSAS* 101 (1972): 127-29.

Sutherland, C.H.V. *Coinage and Currency in Roman Britain*. Oxford: Oxford Univ. Press, 1937. Repr. 1979.

Swan, Vivien G. *The Pottery Kilns of Roman Britain*. London: HMSO, 1984.

—. *Pottery in Roman Britain*. 4th rev. ed. Aylesbury: Shire, 1988.

Thomas, Charles. "Imported Pottery in Dark-Age Western Britain," *Medieval Archaeology* 3 (1959): 89-111.

—. *The Early Christian Archaeology of North Britain*. London: Oxford Univ. Press, 1971.

—. "Irish colonists in south-west Britain." *World Archaeology* 5 (1973): 5-13.

—. *A Provisional List of Imported Pottery in Post-Roman Western Britain and Ireland*. Truro, Cornwall: Institute of Cornish Studies, 1981.

—. *Christianity in Roman Britain to AD 500*. London: Batsford, 1981.

—. "East and West: Tintagel, Early Mediterranean Imports and the Insular Church." In *The Early Church in Western Britain and Ireland*, ed. S. Pearce, pp. 17-34. BAR British Series No. 102. Oxford: BAR Publishing, 1982.

—. *Exploration of a Drowned Landscape: Archaeology and History of the Isles of Scilly*. London: Batsford, 1985.

—. *Celtic Britain*. London: Thames and Hudson, 1986.

—. "Tintagel Castle." *Antiquity* 62 (1988): 421-34.

—. "Christians, Chapels, Churches and Charters." *Landscape History* 11 (1989): 19-26.

—. "The Context of Tintagel. A New Model for the Diffusion of Post-Roman Mediterranean Imports." *Cornish Archaeology* 27 (1990): 7-25.

—. *Tintagel: Arthur and Archaeology*. London: Batsford, 1993.

Thomas, Charles, ed. *Tintagel Papers*. Cornish Studies Vol. 16. Redruth: Institute of Cornish Studies, 1988.

Todd, Malcolm. *Roman Britain*. Atlantic Highlands, NJ: Humanities Press, 1981.

—. "After the Romans." In *The Making of Britain: The Dark Ages*, ed. L. Smith. London: Macmillan, 1984.

—. *The Coritani*. Gloucester: Sutton, 1991.

—. "The Cities of Roman Britain: After Wheeler." In *Roman Towns: The Wheeler Inheritance*, ed. S. Greep, pp. 5-10. CBA Report No. 93. York: CBA, 1993.

Todd, Malcolm, ed. *Research on Roman Britain 1960-89*. Britannia Monograph Series No. 11. London: Society for the Promotion of Roman Studies, 1989.

Tomlin, R.S.O. "Notitia Dignitatum Omnium, Tam Civilium Quam Militarium." In *Aspects of the 'Notitia'*, ed. R. Goodburn and P. Bartholomew, 189-210. BAR Supp. Ser. No. 15. Oxford: BAR Publishing, 1976.

—. "The Curse Tablets." In *The Temple of Sulis Minerva at Bath: Volume 2*, ed. B. Cunliffe, pp. 59-277. Oxford: Oxford Univ. Committee for Archaeology, 1988

Van Arsdale, R.D. *Celtic Coinage of Britain*. London: Spink, 1989.

Wacher, John S. *The Civitas Capitals of Roman Britain*. Leicester: Leicester Univ. Press, 1966.

—. *The Towns of Roman Britain*. Berkeley, CA: Univ. of Cal. Press, 1974.

—. "Late Roman Developments." In *Studies in the Archaeology and History of Cirencester*, ed. A. McWhirr, pp. 15-18. BAR No. 30. Oxford: BAR Publishing, 1976.

—. *Roman Britain*. London: Dent, 1978.

Wacher, John, ed. *The Roman World*. 2 vols. London: Routledge, 1987.

Wainwright, F.T., ed. *The Problem of the Picts*. Perth: Melven Press, 1955.

Watts, Dorothy. *Christians and Pagans in Roman Britain*. London: Routledge, 1991.

Webster, Graham. *The Cornovii*. London: Duckworth, 1975.

—. "Wroxeter (Viroconium)." In *Fortress into City*, pp. 120-44. London: Batsford, 1988.

Webster, Graham, ed. *Fortress into City: The Consolidation of Roman Britain, First Century AD*. London: Batsford, 1988.

Webster, Graham and Philip Barker. *Wroxeter Roman City*. London: English Heritage, 1991.

Welsby, Derek A. *The Roman Military Defense of the British Provinces in its Later Phases*. BAR British Series No. 101. Oxford: BAR Publishing, 1982.

White, Richard B. "Excavations at Aberffraw, Anglesey, 1973 and 1974." *BBCS* 28 (1979): 319-42.

White, Roger. "Excavations on the Site of the Baths Basilica." In *From Roman 'Virconium' to Medieval Wroxeter*, ed. P. Barker, pp. 3-7. Worcester: West Mercian Archaeological Consultants, Ltd., 1990.

Whittock, Martyn J. *The Origins of England 410-600*. London: Croom Helm, 1986.

Wilson, David M. "Medieval Britain in 1970: Pre-Conquest." *Medieval Archaeology* 15 (1971): 124-135.

Wilson, David M., ed. *The Archaeology of Anglo-Saxon England*. London: Methuen, 1976.

Wilson, P.R. *et al.*, eds. *Settlement and Society in the Roman North*. Bradford, West Yorkshire: Yorkshire Archaeological Society, 1984.

Wood, Ian N. Review of *The Ending of Roman Britain*, by A.S. Esmonde Cleary. In *Britannia* 22 (1991): 313-15.

Woodward, Ann. *English Heritage Book of Shrines and Sacrifice*. London: Batsford/English Heritage, 1992.

Wormald, Patrick *et al.*, eds. *Ideal and Reality in Frankish and Anglo-Saxon Society*. Oxford: Blackwell, 1983.

Zeepvat, R.J. *et al. Roman Milton Keynes*. Aylesbury: Buckinghamshire Archaeological Society, 1987

www.ingramcontent.com/pod-product-compliance
Ingram Content Group UK Ltd.
Pitfield, Milton Keynes, MK11 3LW, UK
UKHW061213180426
11947UKWH00029B/2032